CROCK·POT

◆ THE ORIGINAL SLOW COOKER ◆

Comfort Food
Diet Cookbook

Publications International, Ltd.

Nutritional Analysis: Jacqueline B. Marcus, M.S., R.D., L.D., C.N.S., F.A.D.A.

Every effort has been made to check the accuracy of the nutritional information that appears with each recipe. However, because numerous variables account for a wide range of values for certain foods, nutritive analyses in this book should be consider approximate.

This book is for informational purposes and is not intended to provide medical advice. Neither Publications International, Ltd., nor the author or the publisher take responsibility for any possible consequences from any treatment, procedure, exercise, dietary modification, action or application of medicine or preparation by any person reading or following the information in this publication. The publication of this book does not constitute the practice of medicine, and this book does not attempt to replace your physician or other health care provider. Before undertaking any course of treatment, the author, editors and publisher advise the reader to check with a physician or other health care provider.

Pictured on the front cover (clockwise from top left): Beef, Lentil and Onion Soup (page 67), Black Bean and Turkey Stew (page 71), Curry Chicken with Mango and Red Pepper (page 148), Apple-Cinnamon Breakfast Risotto (page 17) and Hearty Beef Short Ribs (page 80). **Pictured on the back cover:** Golden Harvest Pork Stew (page 116).

ISBN-13: 978-1-4508-0898-9
ISBN-10: 1-4508-0898-0

Library of Congress Control Number: 2010931045

Manufactured in China.

8 7 6 5 4 3 2 1

ℰ Contents

Healthy Eating

Many families look for ways to balance their need to eat healthful, nutritious meals with their desire to eat the hearty, home-style food most familiar to them. This book presents a solution: healthful versions of classic comfort foods made in the **CROCK-POT**® slow cooker.

Eating together at home as a family can nurture relationships and promote quality time. In addition, cooking at home allows you to choose your ingredients and control your portions. The familiar, well-loved recipes in this book prove that you can prepare and eat healthy food without sacrificing good taste. Even better, you can count on your **CROCK-POT**® slow cooker to create the same time-tested, convenient and hassle-free meals it always has.

Whether you're embarking on a new healthy eating plan, or you're looking for some nutritious recipes to add to your repertoire, this book has something for you. The recipes were selected to offer delicious, nutritionally balanced recipes that cooks everywhere can confidently offer to their families.

The Principles of Healthy Eating

Whether you're trying to lose weight, maintain your weight, or just eat better, basic nutrition information is what need under your belt. It's easy to be led astray and ultimately become disappointed by misinformation and diets that make outrageous promises. That's why it is important to learn about the role of nutrients in food and how these nutrients are used in your body. Armed with this knowledge, you can resist the siren call of unhealthy diets and make an informed decision about a healthy eating plan that's right for you.

Nutrition Fundamentals

Most foods contain a combination of three energy-producing nutrients—protein, fat, and carbohydrate. These nutrients are responsible for providing the energy that your body's engine needs to run well, and they are essential to your health. Your body requires all three, as well as vitamins, minerals, and water. Fiber, a type of carbohydrate, and fluids both play important roles in managing your weight, too.

If you're trying to lose weight, you've certainly heard the word calorie. Basically, calorie is another word for energy. There are four sources of calories: the three energy-producing nutrients mentioned above (protein, fat, and carbohydrate) and alcohol. Fiber, although it's a carbohydrate, is not processed by the body and is calorie-free.

Calorie Basics

Weight loss (and weight gain, for that matter) is primarily an issue of calories: how many you consume and how many you expend. If the number of calories you eat and the number of calories you use each day are approximately the same, your weight won't

budge. It's only when you consume fewer calories than you use over a period of time that you will lose weight. And it's only when you eat more calories than you use that you will gain weight.

So what numbers of calories are we talking about? This is the crucial equation: One pound of body weight is equal to 3,500 calories. This means that to lose one pound, you must create a 3,500-calorie shortage by eating fewer calories, burning more calories through physical activity, or a combination of both. The exact opposite is true for weight gain. Sounds like a lot, doesn't it? But it's not really. Gaining a pound is as easy as eating an extra 250 calories a day (for instance, any of these: three chocolate chip cookies, one milk chocolate bar, two ounces cheddar cheese, or a

medium-size bagel) for two weeks or skipping a daily workout without cutting back on eating.

And despite claims from popular diet plans, a calorie is a calorie, whether it comes from protein, fat, or carbohydrate. Any calories eaten that your body doesn't burn for energy are stored as body fat, no matter what kind of food package they came in.

There are a few other factors, in addition to calories, that influence your weight. They are your age, your gender, and your genetic blueprint. Unfortunately, these factors are out of your control. So focus on food intake and physical activity, the areas in which you can have an impact.

Making Smart Choices

Eating right and being physically active go hand in hand with keeping a healthy lifestyle. There are certain guidelines you should follow to keep on top of your healthy habits and reducing your risk of chronic diseases and obesity.

The best way to get a handle on eating right is to balance your meals by eating a variety of foods each day. Your goal should be to:

- Select lean sources of protein—like lean meats and poultry. Also add more fish, beans, legumes, and nuts for additional protein.
- Select fresh fruits and vegetables when you can. Opt for fresh, frozen, canned or dried fruits over fruit juices and choose more dark green or orange vegetables for added nutrition and increased fiber.
- Make half your grains whole. Choose whole grains when possible, when selecting cereals, breads, rice, and pasta. Look for grains that say "whole grains" in the ingredient list. This will also be a fiber boost for you.
- Choose fat-free and low-fat milk and dairy products, like cheese and yogurt. These foods will provide you will all that great nutrition, but without excess fat.

- Know your limits. Look for foods that are low in saturated fats, trans fats, cholesterol, salt (sodium), and added sugars.

Each person should aim for a certain number of calories each day. This particular number is based on your age, sex, activity level, and whether you are seeking to maintain your weight, gain weight or lose weight. Typically 2,000 calories is the general reference number used for the average adult to maintain their weight. If you are seeking to lose a few pounds, you will need to reduce this number of calories.

When choosing foods, whether they be those for meals or for snacks, you should seek out choices that are "nutrient dense" and not "empty-calorie" foods. In other words, you should choose foods that provide you the most nutrition for the number of calories (or food energy) that they provide. Choosing foods with calories as well as adequate vitamins and minerals would definitely be a better choice than one, like a sugary soft drink, that provides only calories from sugar, and no other nutrition value.

Now that you are focusing on the "better" choices, you must also keep in mind the importance of portion

Healthy Eating

sizes. Any food that is eaten in too large a quantity, even a good-for-you food, is not a good choice. In order to balance your meals, you should seek out the variety of foods you need, in recommended portion sizes. Refer to the chart below for some examples.

The Comfort of Food

The process of improving one's diet can seem fairly daunting, even frightening. We hear and see so many messages on the importance of a healthful diet that it's easy to feel overwhelmed by the decision of what to eat. Partly this is because many of the messages we receive about food conflict with one another. But another key factor is the role food plays in our lives.

On a certain level, food plays a basic functional role in our daily lives. There are plenty of scientific studies documenting how many calories a person needs each day, the best sources of those calories, the sorts of nutrients we need to ingest each day, etc. While we certainly need to fuel our bodies, food means much more to us than just fuel. Food provides a much needed emotional contact for most people. A shared dinner is the centerpiece of many families' daily interactions with one another. Comfort food comforts us in these and many other ways.

What Is Comfort Food?

When we connect with our loved ones over specific foods, those foods take on an emotional weight of their own. That's why, even years later

Choose Wisely

Eating the familiar, well-loved recipes in this book can help you keep to a sensible eating plan. Consider the following ways to help create healthier versions of your own favorite **CROCK-POT®** slow cooker recipes.

In general

- Portion sizes are incredibly important. Don't be afraid to measure out portions with measuring cups or an accurate kitchen scale.
- Use high calorie or fatty ingredients sparingly or as garnish. Try sprinkling cheese on top of each

serving, rather than adding cups of it into the recipe itself. You'll still get the flavor, but you'll avoid all of the fat.

Ingredients are important

- Recipes using leaner cuts of meat are great choices to start with. Look for recipes for skinless, boneless white meat cuts of poultry. Beef recipes made with cuts with "loin" or "round" in their names are also good options, as are pork recipes made with boneless "loin" cuts.
- Try substituting equal weights of these boneless

cuts for bone-in or fattier cuts in your favorite recipes.
- Look for reduced-fat and reduced-sodium versions of other commonly used ingredients. For example, almost all of the canned broths and canned beans used in these recipes are either reduced-fat or reduced-sodium versions.
- Packaged and prepared products are convenient, but they are often the source of hidden salt or fat in recipes. Try fresh or frozen alternatives to boxed or canned versions whenever practical.

Relative Serving Sizes

There will be occasions when it may be difficult or impractical to measure your meals with a scale or measuring cups. Learning how to estimate appropriate serving sizes can be tricky, but it's made easier if you learn to approximate relative sizes like those in this list:

Fruits
- 1 cup cut-up fruit = closed fist
- ½ cup grapes or berries = light bulb
- 1 medium apple, orange, pear, etc. = baseball

Vegetables
- 1 cup baby carrots = tennis ball
- 1 medium ear of corn = as long as an unsharpened pencil
- 1 cup broccoli florettes = rounded handful

Dairy
- 1 ounce firm cheese (like Cheddar) = 9-volt battery
- 1 cup yogurt or cottage cheese = closed fist
- ½ cup shredded cheese = enough to fill a typical paper cupcake liner

Proteins
- 3 ounces beef or pork = deck of cards or about the size of the palm of your hand
- 3 ounces chicken = average size chicken leg and thigh portion; small chicken breast
- 3 ounces grilled or baked fish fillet = checkbook

Grains and Starches
- ½ cup pasta or rice = typical scoop of ice cream
- 1 ounce bread = typical slice of sandwich bread
- 1 medium potato = computer mouse

Grandma's special Sunday roast recipe reminds us of her and the good times we shared with the whole family. That's one of the most important ways certain foods, comfort foods especially, feed our emotional sides in addition to our physical sides.

For most Americans, "comfort foods" include many of the most classic sorts of **CROCK-POT**® slow cooker foods like pot roast, roasted chicken and potatoes, chicken soup and even spicier fare like chili. Unfortunately, some of the traditional ways of cooking these recipes rely on unhealthy levels of fat and sodium to create the great flavors we remember.

Comfort Food = Diet Food?

The recipes in this book were selected to have fewer calories, fat, sodium, and cholesterol than typical comfort-food recipes. Consider your own dietary needs and calorie allowance for the day when choosing recipes. Refer to the nutritional analysis for each recipe so you have the information to select the recipes that are appropriate for you.

With this book it's simple to plan meals and budget your calories. For example, if you have a higher calorie lunch, select a dinner that's lower in calories to balance out your intake.

Whether you're trying to lose weight, hoping to prevent gaining additional weight, or just looking for ways to eat healthier, the recipes in this book can provide you the heart-warming comfort of your favorite foods, without the fat and calories.

The Joy of Slow Cooking

Slow Cooker Hints and Tips

Slow Cooker Sizes

Smaller slow cookers—such as 1- to 3½-quart models—are the perfect size for cooking for singles, a couple, or empty-nesters (and also for serving dips).

While medium-size slow cookers (those holding somewhere between 3 quarts and 5 quarts) will easily cook enough food at a time to feed a small family, they're also convenient for holiday side dishes or appetizers.

Large slow cookers are great for large family dinners, holiday entertaining, and potluck suppers. A 6-quart to 7-quart model is ideal if you like to make meals in advance, or have dinner tonight and store leftovers for another day.

Types of Slow Cookers

Current **CROCK-POT**® slow cookers come equipped with many different features and benefits, from auto cook programs to stovetop-safe stoneware to timed programming. Visit **www.crockpot.com** to find the slow cooker that best suits your needs.

How you plan to use a slow cooker may affect the model you choose to purchase. For everyday cooking, choose a size large enough to serve your family. If you plan to use the slow cooker primarily for entertaining, choose one of the larger sizes. Basic slow cookers can hold as little as 16 ounces or as much as 7 quarts. The smallest sizes are great for keeping dips hot on a buffet, while the larger sizes can more readily fit large quantities of food and larger roasts.

Cooking, Stirring, and Food Safety

CROCK-POT® slow cookers are safe to leave unattended. The outer heating base may get hot as it cooks, but it should not pose a fire hazard. The heating element in the heating base functions at a low wattage and is safe for your countertops.

The Joy of Slow Cooking

Your slow cooker should be filled about one-half to three-fourths full for most recipes unless otherwise instructed. Lean meats such as chicken or pork tenderloin will cook faster than meats with more connective tissue and fat such as beef chuck or pork shoulder. Bone-in meats will take longer than boneless cuts. Typical slow cooker dishes take approximately 7 to 8 hours to reach the simmer point on LOW and about 3 to 4 hours on HIGH. Once the vegetables and meat start to simmer and braise, their flavors will fully blend and meat will become fall-off-the-bone tender.

According to the USDA, all bacteria are killed at a temperature of 165°F. It is important to follow the recommended cooking times and not to open the lid often, especially early in the cooking process when heat is building up inside the unit. If you need to open the lid to check on your food or are adding additional ingredients, remember to allow additional cooking time if necessary to ensure food is cooked through and tender.

Large slow cookers, the 6- to 7-quart sizes, may benefit with a quick stir halfway during cook time to help distribute heat and promote even cooking. It's usually unnecessary to stir at all, as even ½ cup liquid will help to distribute heat, and the crockery is the perfect medium for holding food at an even temperature throughout the cooking process.

Oven-Safe

All **CROCK-POT®** slow cooker removable crockery inserts may (without their lids) be used safely in ovens at up to 400°F. Also, all **CROCK-POT®** slow cookers are microwavable without their lids. If you own another brand slow cooker, please refer to your owner's manual for specific crockery cooking medium tolerances.

Frozen Food

Frozen food or partially frozen food can be successfully cooked in a slow cooker; however, it will require longer cooking than the same recipe made with fresh food. It's almost always preferable to thaw frozen food prior to placing it in the slow cooker. Using an instant-read thermometer is recommended to ensure meat is fully cooked through.

Pasta and Rice

If you're converting a recipe that calls for uncooked pasta, cook the pasta on the stovetop just until slightly tender before adding to the slow cooker. If you are converting a recipe that calls for cooked rice, stir in raw rice with other ingredients; add ¼ cup extra liquid per ¼ cup of raw rice.

Beans

Beans must be softened completely before combining with sugar and/or acidic foods. Sugar and acid have a hardening effect on beans and will prevent softening. Fully cooked canned beans may be used as a substitute for dried beans.

Vegetables

Root vegetables often cook more slowly than meat.

The Joy of Slow Cooking

Cut vegetables accordingly to cook at the same rate as meat—large or small, or lean versus marbled—and place near the sides or bottom of the stoneware to facilitate cooking.

Herbs

Fresh herbs add flavor and color when added at the end of the cooking cycle; if added at the beginning, many fresh herbs' flavor will dissipate over long cook times. Ground and/or dried herbs and spices work well in slow cooking and may be added at the beginning, and for dishes with shorter cook times, hearty fresh herbs such as rosemary and thyme hold up well. The flavor power of all herbs and spices can vary greatly depending on their particular strength and shelf life. Use chili powders and garlic powder sparingly, as these can sometimes intensify over the long cook times.

Always taste dish at end of cook cycle and correct seasonings including salt and pepper.

Liquids

It is not necessary to use more than ½ to 1 cup liquid in most instances since juices in meats and vegetables are retained more in slow cooking than in conventional cooking. Excess liquid can be cooked down and concentrated after slow cooking on the stovetop or by removing meat and vegetables from stoneware, stirring in one of the following thickeners, and setting the slow cooker to HIGH. Cook on HIGH for approximately 15 minutes until juices are thickened.

Flour: All-purpose flour is often used to thicken soups or stews. Place flour in a small bowl or cup and stir in enough cold water to make a thin, lump-free

stir this mixture into the liquid in the slow cooker. Arrowroot thickens below the boiling point, so it even works well in a slow cooker on LOW. Too much stirring can break down an arrowroot mixture.

Tapioca: Tapioca is a starchy substance extracted from the root of the cassava plant. Its greatest advantage is that it withstands long cooking, making it an ideal choice for slow cooking. Add it at the beginning of cooking and you'll get a clear thickened sauce in the finished dish. Dishes using tapioca as a thickener are best cooked on the LOW setting; tapioca may become stringy when boiled for a long time.

Milk

Milk, cream, and sour cream break down during extended cooking. When possible, add during the last 15 to 30 minutes of cooking, until just heated through. Condensed soups may be substituted for milk and can cook for extended times.

Fish

Fish is delicate and should be stirred in gently during the last 15 to 30 minutes of cooking time. Cook until just cooked through and serve immediately.

Baked Goods

If you wish to prepare bread, cakes, or pudding cakes in a slow cooker, you may want to purchase a covered, vented metal cake pan accessory for your slow cooker. You can also use any straight-sided soufflé dish or deep cake pan that will fit into the ceramic insert of your unit. Baked goods can be prepared directly in the insert; however, they can be a little difficult to remove from the insert, so follow the recipe directions carefully.

mixture. With the slow cooker on HIGH, quickly stir the flour mixture into the liquid in the slow cooker. Cook, stirring frequently, until the mixture thickens.

Cornstarch: Cornstarch gives sauces a clear, shiny appearance; it is used most often for sweet dessert sauces and stir-fry sauces. Place cornstarch in a small bowl or cup and stir in cold water, stirring until the cornstarch dissolves. Quickly stir this mixture into the liquid in the slow cooker; the sauce will thicken as soon as the liquid boils. Cornstarch breaks down with too much heat, so never add it at the beginning of the slow cooking process, and turn off the heat as soon as the sauce thickens.

Arrowroot: Arrowroot (or arrowroot flour) comes from the root of a tropical plant that is dried and ground to a powder; it produces a thick clear sauce. Those who are allergic to wheat often use it in place of flour. Place arrowroot in a small bowl or cup and stir in cold water until the mixture is smooth. Quickly

Breakfast

Apple-Cinnamon Breakfast Risotto

- **3 tablespoons unsalted butter**
- **4 medium Granny Smith apples (about 1½ pounds), peeled, cored and diced into ½-inch cubes**
- **1½ teaspoons ground cinnamon**
- **¼ teaspoon ground allspice**
- **¼ teaspoon salt**
- **1½ cups arborio rice**
- **½ cup packed dark brown sugar**
- **4 cups unfiltered apple juice, at room temperature***
- **1 teaspoon vanilla**
- **Optional toppings: dried cranberries, sliced almonds, milk**

*If unfiltered apple juice is unavailable, use any apple juice.

> **Tip**
> Keep the lid on! The **CROCK-POT®** slow cooker can take as long as 30 minutes to regain heat lost when the cover is removed.

1. Coat **CROCK-POT®** slow cooker with nonstick cooking spray; set aside. Melt butter in large skillet over medium-high heat. Add apples, cinnamon, allspice and salt. Cook and stir 3 to 5 minutes or until apples begin to release juices. Transfer to **CROCK-POT®** slow cooker.

2. Add rice and stir to coat. Sprinkle brown sugar evenly over top. Add apple juice and vanilla. Cover; cook on HIGH 1½ to 2 hours or until all liquid is absorbed. Ladle risotto into bowls and serve hot. Garnish as desired.

Makes 6 servings

Nutrition Information: Serving Size about 1¼ cups, Calories 342, Total Fat 6g, Saturated Fat 4g, Protein 2g, Carbohydrate 72g, Cholesterol 15mg, Dietary Fiber 4g, Sodium 123mg

Breakfast

Bran Muffin Bread

2	cups all-bran cereal
2	cups whole wheat flour*
2	teaspoons baking powder
1	teaspoon baking soda
¼	teaspoon ground cinnamon
½	teaspoon salt
1	egg
1½	cups buttermilk
¼	cup molasses
¼	cup (½ stick) unsalted butter, melted
1	cup chopped walnuts
½	cup raisins

For proper texture of finished bread, spoon flour into measuring cup and level off. Do not dip into bag, pack down flour or tap on counter to level when measuring.

1. Generously butter and flour 8-cup mold that fits into 6-quart **CROCK-POT®** slow cooker; set aside. Combine cereal, flour, baking powder, baking soda, cinnamon and salt in large bowl. Stir to blend well.

2. Beat egg in medium bowl. Add buttermilk, molasses and melted butter. Mix well to blend. Add to flour mixture. Stir only until ingredients are combined. Stir in walnuts and raisins. Spoon batter into prepared mold. Cover with buttered foil, butter side down.

3. Place rack in **CROCK-POT®** slow cooker or prop up mold with a few equal-size potatoes. Pour 1 inch hot water into **CROCK-POT®** slow cooker (water should not come to top of rack). Place mold on rack. Cover; cook on LOW 3½ to 4 hours.

4. To check for doneness, lift foil. Bread should just start to pull away from sides of mold, and toothpick inserted into center of bread should come out clean. If necessary, replace foil and continue cooking 45 minutes longer.

5. Remove mold from **CROCK-POT®** slow cooker. Let stand 10 minutes. Remove foil and run rubber spatula around outer edges, lifting bottom slightly to loosen. Invert bread onto wire rack. Cool until lukewarm. Slice and serve with honey butter, if desired.

Makes 12 servings

Nutrition Information: Serving Size 1 slice (½2 loaf), Calories 258, Total Fat 12g, Saturated Fat 4g, Protein 8g, Carbohydrate 36g, Cholesterol 31mg, Dietary Fiber 6g, Sodium 356mg

Orange Date-Nut Bread

   2 **cups unbleached all-purpose flour**

 ½ **cup chopped pecans**

   1 **teaspoon baking powder**

 ½ **teaspoon baking soda**

 ¼ **teaspoon salt**

   1 **cup chopped dates**

   2 **teaspoons dried orange peel**

 ⅔ **cup boiling water**

 ¾ **cup sugar**

   2 **tablespoons shortening**

   1 **egg, lightly beaten**

   1 **teaspoon vanilla**

Variation
Substitute 1 cup dried cranberries for dates.

1. Spray 1-quart casserole, soufflé dish or other high-sided baking pan with nonstick cooking spray; dust with flour. Set aside.

2. Combine flour, pecans, baking powder, baking soda and salt in medium bowl; set aside.

3. Combine dates and orange peel in separate medium bowl; pour boiling water over date mixture. Add sugar, shortening, egg and vanilla; stir just until blended.

4. Add flour mixture to date mixture; stir just until blended. Pour batter into prepared dish; place in 4½-quart **CROCK-POT**® slow cooker. Cover; cook on HIGH about 2½ hours or until edges begin to brown.

5. Remove dish. Cool on wire rack about 10 minutes; remove bread from dish and cool completely on rack.

Makes 10 servings

Nutrition Information: Serving Size 1 slice (⅒ loaf), Calories 365, Total Fat 7g, Saturated Fat 1g, Protein 8g, Carbohydrate 48g, Cholesterol 22mg, Dietary Fiber 2g, Sodium 490mg

Ham and Cheddar Brunch Strata

  8 **ounces French bread, torn into small pieces**

1¾ **cups shredded reduced-fat sharp Cheddar cheese, divided**

  1 **cup diced lean ham**

½ **cup finely chopped green onions (white and green parts), divided**

  4 **large eggs**

  1 **cup fat-free half-and-half**

  1 **tablespoon Worcestershire sauce**

⅛ **teaspoon ground red pepper**

Tip

When preparing ingredients for the **CROCK-POT**® slow cooker, cut into uniform pieces so everything cooks evenly.

1. Coat **CROCK-POT**® slow cooker with nonstick cooking spray. Cut parchment paper to fit bottom of stoneware* and press into place. Spray paper lightly with nonstick cooking spray.

2. Layer in following order: bread, 1½ cups cheese, ham and all but 2 tablespoons green onions.

3. Whisk eggs, half-and-half, Worcestershire sauce and red pepper in small bowl. Pour evenly over layered ingredients in **CROCK-POT**® slow cooker. Cover; cook on LOW 3½ hours or until knife inserted into center comes out clean. Turn off heat. Sprinkle evenly with reserved ½ cup cheese and 2 tablespoons green onions. Let stand, covered, 10 minutes or until cheese has melted.

4. To serve, run a knife or rubber spatula around outer edges, lifting bottom slightly. Invert onto plate and peel off paper. Invert again onto serving plate.

To cut parchment paper to fit, trace around the stoneware bottom, then cut the paper slightly smaller to fit. If parchment paper is unavailable, substitute waxed paper.

Makes 8 servings

Nutrition Information: Serving Size about 1 cup, Calories 273, Total Fat 10g, Saturated Fat 4g, Protein 19g, Carbohydrate 28g, Cholesterol 142mg, Dietary Fiber 1g, Sodium 562mg

Glazed Orange Poppy Seed Cake

Batter

1½ **cups biscuit baking mix**

¾ **cup granulated sugar**

2 **tablespoons poppy seeds**

½ **cup sour cream**

1 **egg**

2 **tablespoons 2% milk**

1 **teaspoon vanilla**

2 **teaspoons orange zest**

Glaze

¼ **cup orange juice**

2 **cups powdered sugar, sifted**

2 **teaspoons poppy seeds**

1. Coat inside of 4-quart **CROCK-POT**® slow cooker with nonstick cooking spray. Cut waxed paper circle to fit bottom of **CROCK-POT**® slow cooker (trace insert bottom and cut slightly smaller to fit). Spray lightly with cooking spray.

2. Whisk together baking mix, granulated sugar and poppy seeds in medium bowl; set aside. In another bowl, blend sour cream, egg, milk, vanilla and orange zest. Whisk wet ingredients into dry mixture until thoroughly blended.

3. Spoon batter into prepared **CROCK-POT**® slow cooker and smooth top. Place paper towel under lid, then cover. Cook on HIGH 1 hour 30 minutes. (Cake is done when top is no longer shiny and a toothpick inserted in center comes out clean.)

4. Invert cake onto cooling rack, peel off waxed paper and allow to cool (right side up) on cooling rack.

5. Whisk orange juice into powdered sugar. Cut cake into 8 wedges and place on cooling rack with a tray underneath to catch drips. With a small spatula or knife, spread glaze over top and cut sides of each wedge. Sprinkle poppy seeds over wedges and allow glaze to set.

Makes 8 servings

Nutrition Information: Serving Size 1 slice (⅛ cake), Calories 342, Total Fat 7g, Saturated Fat 3g, Protein 4g, Carbohydrate 66g, Cholesterol 37mg, Dietary Fiber 0g, Sodium 475mg

Glazed Cinnamon Coffee Cake

Streusel

- ¼ **cup biscuit baking mix**
- ¼ **cup packed light brown sugar**
- ½ **teaspoon ground cinnamon**

Batter

- 1½ **cups biscuit baking mix**
- ¾ **cup granulated sugar**
- ½ **cup unflavored yogurt**
- 1 **large egg, lightly beaten**
- 1 **teaspoon vanilla**

Glaze

- 2 **tablespoons 2% milk**
- 1 **cup powdered sugar**
- ½ **cup sliced almonds (optional)**

> **Note**
> This recipe works best in a round **CROCK-POT®** slow cooker.

1. Generously coat 4-quart **CROCK-POT®** slow cooker with butter or cooking spray. Cut parchment paper to fit bottom of stoneware* and press into place. Spray paper lightly with nonstick cooking spray.

2. Prepare streusel: Blend ¼ cup baking mix, brown sugar and cinnamon in small bowl; set aside.

3. Prepare batter: Mix 1½ cups baking mix, granulated sugar, yogurt, egg and vanilla in medium bowl until well blended. Spoon ½ of batter into **CROCK-POT®** slow cooker. Sprinkle ½ of streusel over top. Repeat with remaining batter and streusel.

4. Line lid with 2 paper towels. Cover tightly; cook on HIGH 1¾ to 2 hours or until tester inserted in center comes out clean and cake springs back when gently pressed. Allow cake to rest 10 minutes. Invert onto plate and peel off paper. Invert again onto serving plate.

5. Prepare glaze: Whisk milk into powdered sugar, 1 tablespoon at a time, until desired consistency. Spoon glaze over top of cake. Garnish with sliced almonds, if desired. Cut into wedges. Serve warm or cold.

To cut parchment paper to fit, trace around the stoneware bottom, then cut the paper slightly smaller to fit. If parchment paper is unavailable, substitute waxed paper.

Makes 8 servings

Nutrition Information: Serving Size 1 slice (⅛ cake), Calories 283, Total Fat 4g, Saturated Fat 1g, Protein 4g, Carbohydrate 60g, Cholesterol 28mg, Dietary Fiber 0g, Sodium 404mg

Breakfast

Whole-Grain Banana Bread

¼ **cup plus 2 tablespoons wheat germ, divided**

½ **cup (1 stick) unsalted light butter, softened**

1 **cup sugar**

2 **eggs**

3 **medium bananas, mashed (about 1 cup)**

1 **teaspoon vanilla**

1 **cup all-purpose flour**

1 **cup whole wheat pastry flour**

1 **teaspoon baking soda**

½ **teaspoon salt**

½ **cup chopped walnuts or pecans (optional)**

1. Spray 1-quart casserole, soufflé dish or other high-sided baking pan with nonstick cooking spray. Sprinkle dish with 2 tablespoons wheat germ.

2. Beat butter and sugar in large bowl with electric mixer until fluffy. Add eggs, one at a time; beat until blended. Add bananas and vanilla; beat until smooth.

3. Gradually stir in flours, remaining ¼ cup wheat germ, baking soda and salt. Stir in nuts, if desired. Pour batter into prepared dish; place in 4½-quart **CROCK-POT**® slow cooker. Cover; cook on LOW 4 to 6 hours or on HIGH 2 to 3 hours or until edges begin to brown and toothpick inserted into center comes out clean.

4. Remove dish from **CROCK-POT**® slow cooker. Cool on wire rack about 10 minutes. Remove bread from dish; cool completely on wire rack.

Makes 10 servings

Nutrition Information: Serving Size 1 slice (¹⁄₁₀ loaf), Calories 285, Total Fat 8g, Saturated Fat 4g, Protein 6g, Carbohydrate 49g, Cholesterol 55mg, Dietary Fiber 4g, Sodium 419mg

Cheese Grits with Chiles and Bacon

- **3 strips turkey bacon, divided**
- **1 jalapeño pepper, cored, seeded and minced***
- **1 small yellow onion, finely chopped**
- **1 cup grits****
- **4 cups 99% fat-free, sodium-free chicken broth**
- **¼ teaspoon black pepper**
- **Salt, to taste**
- **½ cup fat-free half-and-half**
- **1 cup shredded reduced-fat sharp Cheddar cheese**
- **2 tablespoons finely chopped green onion, green part only**

*Hot peppers can sting and irritate the skin, so wear rubber gloves when handling peppers and do not touch your eyes.

**You may use coarse, instant, yellow or stone-ground grits.

1. Fry bacon on both sides in medium skillet until crisp. Remove bacon and drain on paper towels. Cut 2 strips into bite-size pieces. Refrigerate and reserve remaining bacon. Place cut-up bacon in **CROCK-POT®** slow cooker.

2. Drain all but 1 tablespoon bacon drippings in skillet.
Add pepper and onion. Cook and stir over medium-high heat 1 minute or until onion is transparent and lightly browned. Transfer to **CROCK-POT®** slow cooker. Stir in grits, broth, pepper and salt. Cover; cook on LOW 4 hours.

3. Stir in half-and-half and cheese. Sprinkle on green onion. Chop remaining bacon into bite-size pieces and stir into grits or sprinkle on top of each serving. Serve immediately.

Makes 4 servings

Nutrition Information: Serving Size about 1¼ cups, Calories 305, Total Fat 11g, Saturated Fat 5g, Protein 8g, Carbohydrate 6g, Cholesterol 60mg, Dietary Fiber 1g, Sodium 605mg

Breakfast

Breakfast Berry Bread Pudding

- **6 cups bread, preferably dense peasant-style or sourdough, cut into ¾- to 1-inch cubes**
- **½ cup slivered almonds, toasted***
- **1 cup raisins**
- **6 large eggs, beaten**
- **1¾ cups 1% milk**
- **1 teaspoon vanilla**
- **1½ cups packed light brown sugar**
- **1½ teaspoons ground cinnamon**
- **3 cups sliced fresh strawberries**
- **2 cups fresh blueberries**
- **Fresh mint leaves (optional)**

To toast almonds, spread in single layer in heavy-bottomed skillet. Cook over medium heat 1 to 2 minutes, stirring frequently, until nuts are lightly browned. Remove from skillet immediately. Cool before using.

1. Coat **CROCK-POT®** slow cooker with nonstick cooking spray or butter. Add bread, almonds and raisins, and toss to combine.

2. Whisk together eggs, milk, vanilla, brown sugar and cinnamon in separate bowl. Pour egg mixture over bread mixture; toss to blend. Cover; cook on LOW 4 to 4½ hours or on HIGH 3 hours.

3. Remove stoneware from **CROCK-POT®** base and allow bread pudding to cool and set before serving. Serve with berries and garnish with mint leaves, if desired.

Makes 12 servings

Nutrition Information: Serving Size about 1 cup, Calories 300, Total Fat 6g, Saturated Fat 1g, Protein 7g, Carbohydrate 57g, Cholesterol 109mg, Dietary Fiber 3g, Sodium 179mg

Breakfast

Honey Whole-Grain Bread

- **3 cups whole wheat bread flour, divided**
- **2 cups warm (not hot) whole milk**
- **¾ cup all-purpose flour, divided**
- **¼ cup honey**
- **2 tablespoons vegetable oil**
- **1 package active dry yeast**
- **¾ teaspoon salt**

1. Make foil handles using three 18 × 2-inch strips of heavy-duty foil, or use regular foil folded to double thickness. Place in stoneware; crisscross foil to form spoke design across bottom and up sides. Prepare 1-quart casserole, soufflé dish or other high-sided baking pan that will fit in 4½-quart **CROCK-POT®** slow cooker by coating with nonstick cooking spray; set aside.

2. Combine 1½ cups whole wheat flour, milk, ½ cup all-purpose flour, honey, oil, yeast and salt in large bowl. Beat with electric mixer at medium speed 2 minutes. Add remaining 1½ cups whole wheat flour and ¼ cup to ½ cup all-purpose flour until dough is no longer sticky. (If mixer has difficulty mixing dough, mix in remaining flours with wooden spoon.) Transfer to prepared casserole.

3. Place casserole in **CROCK-POT®** slow cooker. Cover; cook on HIGH 3 hours or until edges are browned.

4. Use foil handles to lift dish from **CROCK-POT®** slow cooker. Let stand 5 minutes. Unmold on wire rack to cool.

Makes 10 servings

Nutrition Information: Serving Size 1 slice (1/10 loaf), Calories 237, Total Fat 5g, Saturated Fat 1g, Protein 8g, Carbohydrate 42g, Cholesterol 5mg, Dietary Fiber 5g, Sodium 316mg

Breakfast

Whoa Breakfast

- **1½ cups steel-cut or old-fashioned oats**
- **3 cups water**
- **2 cups chopped peeled apples**
- **¼ cup sliced almonds**
- **½ teaspoon ground cinnamon**

Combine oats, water, apples, almonds and cinnamon in **CROCK-POT®** slow cooker. Cover; cook on LOW 8 hours.

Makes 6 servings

Nutrition Information: Serving Size about 1 cup, Calories 124, Total Fat 3g, Saturated Fat 0g, Protein 4g, Carbohydrate 20g, Cholesterol 0mg, Dietary Fiber 4g, Sodium 5mg

Hawaiian Fruit Compote

- 3 **cups coarsely chopped fresh pineapple**
- 3 **grapefruits, peeled and sectioned**
- 2 **cups chopped fresh peaches**
- 2 **to 3 limes, peeled and sectioned**
- 1 **mango, peeled and chopped**
- 2 **bananas, peeled and sliced**
- 1 **tablespoon lemon juice**
- 1 **can (21 ounces) cherry pie filling**
  Slivered almonds (optional)

1. Place all ingredients except almonds in **CROCK-POT**® slow cooker and toss lightly. Cover; cook on LOW 4 to 5 hours or on HIGH 2 to 3 hours.

2. Serve with slivered almonds, if desired.

Makes 8 servings

Nutrition Information: Serving Size about 1 cup, Calories 225, Total Fat 0g, Saturated Fat 0g, Protein 2g, Carbohydrate 58g, Cholesterol 0mg, Dietary Fiber 8g, Sodium 15mg

Serving Suggestion

Try warm, fruity compote in place of maple syrup on your favorite pancakes or waffles for a great way to start your day. This sauce is also delicious served over roasted turkey, pork roast or baked ham.

Mucho Mocha Cocoa

- **1 cup chocolate syrup**
- **⅓ cup instant coffee granules**
- **2 tablespoons sugar**
- **1 teaspoon ground cinnamon**
- **1 quart 2% milk**
- **1 quart fat-free half-and-half**

Tip

This is great for a party. If desired, add 1 ounce of rum or whiskey to each serving.

Combine all ingredients in **CROCK-POT®** slow cooker. Stir until well blended. Cover and cook on LOW 3 hours. Serve hot in mugs.

Makes 9 servings

Nutrition Information: Serving Size about 1 cup, Calories 229, Total Fat 4g, Saturated Fat 2g, Protein 7g, Carbohydrate 41g, Cholesterol 14mg, Dietary Fiber 1g, Sodium 230mg

Pear Crunch

   1   **can (8 ounces) crushed pineapple in juice, undrained**
   ¼   **cup pineapple or apple juice**
   3   **tablespoons dried cranberries**
   1½ **teaspoons quick-cooking tapioca**
   ¼   **teaspoon vanilla**
   2   **pears, cored and cut into halves**
   ¼   **cup granola with almonds**
       Mint leaves (optional)

1. Combine undrained pineapple, juice, cranberries, tapioca and vanilla in **CROCK-POT**® slow cooker; mix well. Place pears cut side down on pineapple mixture.

2. Cover; cook on LOW 3½ to 4½ hours. Arrange pear halves on serving plates. Spoon pineapple mixture over pear halves. Garnish with granola and mint leaves, if desired.

Makes 4 servings

Nutrition Information: Serving Size about 1 cup, Calories 150, Total Fat 2g, Saturated Fat 0g, Protein 1g, Carbohydrate 35g, Cholesterol 0mg, Dietary Fiber 4g, Sodium 4mg

Apple and Granola Breakfast Cobbler

    4 medium Granny Smith apples, peeled, cored and sliced

  ½ **cup packed light brown sugar**

    1 teaspoon ground cinnamon

    1 tablespoon lemon juice

    2 tablespoons butter, cut into small pieces

    2 cups granola cereal, plus additional for garnish

       Cream, half-and-half or vanilla yogurt (optional)

1. Place apples in **CROCK-POT®** slow cooker. Sprinkle brown sugar, cinnamon and lemon juice over apples. Stir in butter and granola.

2. Cover; cook on LOW 6 hours or on HIGH 2 to 3 hours. Serve hot with additional granola sprinkled on top. Serve with cream, if desired.

Makes 4 servings

Nutrition Information: Serving Size about 1 cup, Calories 393, Total Fat 11g, Saturated Fat 4g, Protein 5g, Carbohydrate 73g, Cholesterol 15mg, Dietary Fiber 8g, Sodium 30mg

Chai Tea

2	**quarts (8 cups) water**
8	**bags black tea**
¾	**cup sugar***
2	**teaspoons ground cloves**
2½	**teaspoons ground cardamom (optional)**
2½	**teaspoons ground cinnamon**
8	**slices fresh ginger**
1	**cup 2% milk**

*Chai tea is typically sweet. For less-sweet tea, reduce sugar to ½ cup.

1. Combine water, tea, sugar, cloves, cardamom, if desired, cinnamon and ginger in **CROCK-POT®** slow cooker. Cover; cook on HIGH 2 to 2½ hours.

2. Strain mixture; discard solids. (At this point, tea may be covered and refrigerated up to 3 days.)

3. Stir in milk just before serving. Serve warm or chilled.

Makes 10 servings

Nutrition Information: Serving Size 1 scant cup, Calories 77, Total Fat 1g, Saturated Fat 0g, Protein 1g, Carbohydrate 18g, Cholesterol 2mg, Dietary Fiber 1g, Sodium 21mg

Bacon and Cheese Brunch Potatoes

- 3 **medium russet potatoes (about 2 pounds), unpeeled and cut into 1-inch dice**
- 1 **cup chopped onion**
- ½ **teaspoon seasoned salt**
- 4 **slices crisply cooked bacon, crumbled**
- 1 **cup (4 ounces) shredded sharp Cheddar cheese**
- 1 **tablespoon water**

1. Coat **CROCK-POT®** slow cooker with cooking spray. Place half of potatoes in **CROCK-POT®** slow cooker. Sprinkle ½ of onion and seasoned salt over potatoes; top with ½ of bacon and cheese. Repeat layers, ending with cheese. Sprinkle water over top.

2. Cover; cook on LOW 6 hours or on HIGH 3½ hours, or until potatoes and onion are tender. Stir gently to mix and serve hot.

Makes 6 servings

Nutrition Information: Serving Size about 1 cup, Calories 197, Total Fat 8g, Saturated Fat 4g, Protein 9g, Carbohydrate 22g, Cholesterol 26mg, Dietary Fiber 2g, Sodium 379mg

Cinnamon Latté

6 cups double-strength brewed coffee*

2 cups half-and-half

1 cup sugar

1 teaspoon vanilla

1½ teaspoons ground cinnamon

Whipped cream (optional)

Cinnamon sticks (optional)

Double the amount of coffee grounds normally used to brew coffee. Or, substitute 8 teaspoons instant coffee dissolved in 6 cups boiling water.

Blend coffee, half-and-half, sugar and vanilla in 3- to 4-quart **CROCK-POT®** slow cooker. Add cinnamon. Cover; cook on HIGH 3 hours. Serve in tall coffee mugs topped with whipped cream and garnished with cinnamon stick, if desired.

Makes 8 servings

Nutrition Information: Serving Size 1 cup, Calories 180, Total Fat 7g, Saturated Fat 4g, Protein 2g, Carbohydrate 28g, Cholesterol 22mg, Dietary Fiber 0g, Sodium 29mg

Chilies, Soups & Stews

Chili with Turkey & Beans

- 2 **cans (14 ounces each) sodium-free, peeled whole tomatoes, drained**
- 2 **cans (14 ounces each) sodium-free red kidney beans, rinsed and drained**
- 1 **pound cooked 99% fat-free ground turkey**
- 1 **can (14 ounces) reduced-sodium black beans, rinsed and drained**
- 1 **can (12 ounces) sodium-free tomato sauce**
- 1 **cup finely chopped yellow onion**
- 1 **cup finely chopped celery**
- 1 **cup finely chopped carrot**
- 3 **tablespoons chili powder**
- 1 **tablespoon Worcestershire sauce**
- 4 **teaspoons ground cumin**
- 2 **teaspoons ground red pepper**
- 1 **teaspoon salt**
- ½ **cup amaretto (optional)**

Combine all ingredients in **CROCK-POT®** slow cooker. Cover; cook on HIGH 7 hours.

Makes 6 servings

Nutrition Information: Serving Size about 1¼ cups, Calories 301, Total Fat 2g, Saturated Fat 0g, Protein 33g, Carbohydrate 43g, Cholesterol 30mg, Dietary Fiber 18g, Sodium 771mg

Chinese Chicken Stew

- 1 **pound boneless, skinless chicken thighs, cut into 1-inch pieces**
- 1 **teaspoon Chinese five-spice powder***
- ½ **teaspoon red pepper flakes**
- 1 **tablespoon vegetable oil**
- 1 **large yellow onion, coarsely chopped**
- 1 **package (8 ounces) fresh mushrooms, sliced**
- 2 **cloves garlic, minced**
- 1 **can (about 14 ounces) 99% fat-free chicken broth, divided**
- 1 **tablespoon cornstarch**
- 1 **large red bell pepper, cut into ¾-inch pieces**
- 2 **tablespoons soy sauce**
- 2 **large green onions, cut into ½-inch pieces**
- 1 **tablespoon sesame oil**
- 3 **cups hot cooked white rice (optional)**
- ¼ **cup coarsely chopped fresh cilantro (optional)**

Chinese five-spice powder is a blend of cinnamon, cloves, fennel seed, anise and Szechuan peppercorns. It is available in most supermarkets and at Asian grocery stores.

1. Toss chicken with five-spice powder and red pepper flakes in small bowl. Heat vegetable oil in large skillet. Add onion and chicken; cook and stir about 5 minutes or until chicken is browned. Add mushrooms and garlic; cook and stir until chicken is no longer pink.

2. Combine ¼ cup broth and cornstarch in small bowl; set aside. Place cooked chicken mixture, remaining broth, bell pepper and soy sauce in **CROCK-POT**® slow cooker. Cover; cook on LOW 3½ hours or until peppers are tender.

3. Stir in cornstarch mixture, green onions and sesame oil. Cook 30 to 45 minutes or until thickened. Ladle into soup bowls; scoop ½ cup rice into each bowl and sprinkle with cilantro, if desired.

Makes 6 servings

Nutrition Information: Serving Size about 1 cup, Calories 172, Total Fat 10g, Saturated Fat 3g, Protein 17g, Carbohydrate 9g, Cholesterol 61mg, Dietary Fiber 1g, Sodium 759mg

Asian Beef Stew

- 1½ pounds round steak, thinly sliced
- 2 medium yellow onions, cut into ¼-inch slices
- 2 stalks celery, sliced
- 2 carrots, peeled and sliced *or* 1 cup baby carrots
- 1 cup sliced mushrooms
- 1 cup orange juice
- 1 cup beef broth
- ⅓ cup hoisin sauce
- 2 tablespoons cornstarch
- 1 to 2 teaspoons Chinese five-spice powder *or* curry powder
- 1 cup frozen peas, thawed

  Hot cooked rice

  Chopped fresh cilantro (optional)

1. Place beef, onions, celery, carrots and mushrooms in **CROCK-POT®** slow cooker.

2. Blend orange juice, broth, hoisin sauce, cornstarch and five-spice powder in small bowl. Pour into **CROCK-POT®** slow cooker. Cover; cook on LOW 6 to 8 hours or on HIGH 5 hours or until beef is tender.

3. Stir in peas. Cook 20 minutes or until peas are tender. Serve with rice. Garnish with cilantro, if desired.

Makes 6 servings

Nutrition Information: Serving Size 1½ cups, Calories 415, Total Fat 5g, Saturated Fat 2g, Protein 30g, Carbohydrate 59g, Cholesterol 63mg, Dietary Fiber 3g, Sodium 423mg

Chilies, Soups & Stews

Parsnip and Carrot Soup

1 **medium leek, thinly sliced**

Nonstick cooking spray

4 **medium parsnips, peeled and diced**

4 **medium carrots, peeled and diced**

4 **cups 99% fat-free, reduced-sodium chicken broth**

1 **bay leaf**

¼ **teaspoon salt**

½ **teaspoon freshly ground pepper**

2 **ounces small pasta, cooked al denté and drained**

1 **tablespoon chopped Italian parsley**

1 **cup fat-free croutons (optional)**

> ## Note
> This dish is a great year-round accompaniment to a main course of roasted meat. Or, the soup can stand alone as a quick, satisfying meal in its own right.

1. Cook the leek in a small nonstick skillet, sprayed with nonstick cooking spray, over medium heat until golden. Place in the **CROCK-POT®** slow cooker.

2. Add the parsnips, carrots, broth, bay leaf, salt and pepper. Cover; cook on LOW 6 to 9 hours or on HIGH 2 to 4 hours or until the vegetables are tender. Add the pasta during the last hour of cooking.

3. Remove bay leaf. Sprinkle each individual serving with parsley and croutons, if desired.

Makes 4 servings

Nutrition Information: Serving Size about 1½ cups, Calories 196, Total Fat 1g, Saturated Fat 0g, Protein 5g, Carbohydrate 44g, Cholesterol 0mg, Dietary Fiber 9g, Sodium 800mg

Chilies, Soups & Stews

Beef Chuck Chili

- 3 **pounds lean beef chuck roast**
- ¼ **cup olive oil, divided**
- 3 **cups minced yellow onions**
- 4 **poblano peppers, seeded and diced***
- 2 **serrano peppers, seeded and diced***
- 2 **green bell peppers, seeded and diced**
- 3 **jalapeño peppers, seeded and diced****
- 2 **tablespoons minced garlic**
- 1 **can (28 ounces) crushed tomatoes**
- ¼ **cup hot pepper sauce**
- 1 **tablespoon ground cumin**
  Black pepper, to taste
- 4 **ounces Mexican lager beer (optional)**
  Corn bread or hot cooked rice (optional)

Handle fresh chili peppers as directed for jalapeño peppers. If fresh chili peppers are unavailable, use 2 cans (4 ounces each) diced green chiles and add dried ground chili powder for more heat.

**Jalapeño peppers can sting and irritate the skin. Wear rubber gloves when handling peppers and do not touch your eyes. Wash hands after handling peppers.*

1. Trim excess fat from roast and discard. Heat 2 tablespoons olive oil in large skillet over medium-high heat until hot. Add chuck roast; sear on both sides. Transfer beef to **CROCK-POT®** slow cooker.

2. Heat remaining 2 tablespoons oil in same skillet over low heat. Add onions, peppers and garlic; cook and stir about 7 minutes or until onions are tender. Transfer to **CROCK-POT®** slow cooker. Add crushed tomatoes. Cover; cook on LOW 4 to 5 hours or until beef is fork-tender.

3. Remove beef from **CROCK-POT®** slow cooker. Shred beef with 2 forks. Add hot sauce, cumin, black pepper and beer, if desired, to cooking liquid. Return beef to cooking liquid and mix well. Serve over corn bread or rice, if desired.

Makes 10 servings

Nutrition Information: Serving Size about 1 cup, Calories 298, Total Fat 12g, Saturated Fat 3g, Protein 32g, Carbohydrate 14g, Cholesterol 60mg, Dietary Fiber 3g, Sodium 360mg

 **Chilies, Soups & Stews**

Creamy Cauliflower Bisque

- 1 **pound frozen cauliflower florets**
- 1 **pound baking potatoes, peeled and cut into 1-inch cubes**
- 1 **cup chopped yellow onion**
- 2 **cans (about 14 ounces each) fat-free, reduced-sodium chicken broth**
- ½ **teaspoon dried thyme**
- ¼ **teaspoon garlic powder**
- ⅛ **teaspoon ground red pepper**
- 1 **cup evaporated skim milk**
- 2 **tablespoons unsalted butter**
- ½ **teaspoon salt**
- ¼ **teaspoon black pepper**
- 1 **cup (4 ounces) shredded reduced-fat sharp Cheddar cheese**
- ¼ **cup finely chopped parsley**
- ¼ **cup finely chopped green onions**

1. Combine cauliflower, potatoes, onion, broth, thyme, garlic powder and ground red pepper in **CROCK-POT®** slow cooker. Cover; cook on LOW 8 hours, or on HIGH 4 hours.

2. Pour soup in blender in batches; process until smooth, holding lid down firmly. Return puréed batches to slow cooker. Add milk, butter, salt and black pepper; stir until blended.

3. Top individual servings with cheese, parsley and green onions.

Makes 9 servings

Nutrition Information: Serving Size about 1¼ cups, Calories 142, Total Fat 6g, Saturated Fat 3g, Protein 8g, Carbohydrate 17g, Cholesterol 17mg, Dietary Fiber 2g, Sodium 473mg

Chicken Tortilla Soup

1 **pound boneless, skinless chicken breasts**

2 **cans (15 ounces each) diced tomatoes, undrained**

1 **can (4 ounces) chopped mild green chilies, drained**

½ **cup 99% fat-free chicken broth**

1 **medium yellow onion, diced**

2 **cloves garlic, minced**

1 **teaspoon ground cumin**

Salt and black pepper, to taste

4 **corn tortillas, sliced into ¼-inch strips**

2 **tablespoons chopped fresh cilantro**

½ **cup shredded Monterey Jack cheese**

1 **avocado, peeled, diced and tossed with lime juice to prevent browning**

Lime wedges

1. Place chicken in **CROCK-POT®** slow cooker. Combine tomatoes with juice, chilies, broth, onion, garlic and cumin in small bowl. Pour mixture over chicken.

2. Cover; cook on LOW 6 hours or on HIGH 3 hours, or until chicken is tender. Remove chicken from **CROCK-POT®** slow cooker. Shred with 2 forks. Return to cooking liquid. Adjust seasonings, adding salt and pepper and more broth, if necessary.

3. Just before serving, add tortillas and cilantro to **CROCK-POT®** slow cooker. Stir to blend. Serve in soup bowls, topping each serving with cheese, avocado and a squeeze of lime juice.

Makes 6 servings

Nutrition Information: Serving Size about 1¼ cups, Calories 254, Total Fat 10g, Saturated Fat 3g, Protein 22g, Carbohydrate 19g, Cholesterol 57mg, Dietary Fiber 5g, Sodium 573mg

Smoked Sausage and Bean Soup

2	cans (14 ounces each) 99% fat-free chicken broth
1½	cups hot water
1	cup dried black beans, sorted and rinsed
1	cup chopped yellow onion
2	bay leaves
1	teaspoon sugar
⅛	teaspoon ground red pepper
6	ounces reduced-fat smoked sausage
1	cup chopped tomato
1	tablespoon Worcestershire sauce
2	teaspoons extra-virgin olive oil
1	tablespoon chili powder
1½	teaspoons ground cumin
½	teaspoon salt
¼	cup chopped cilantro

1. Combine broth, water, beans, onion, bay leaves, sugar and red pepper in **CROCK-POT®** slow cooker. Cover; cook on LOW 8 hours or on HIGH 4 hours.

2. Coat large skillet with nonstick cooking spray. Heat over medium-high heat until hot. Add sausage and cook until beginning to brown, stirring to break up meat.

3. Add sausage and remaining ingredients except cilantro to **CROCK-POT®** slow cooker. Cover; cook on HIGH 15 minutes to blend flavors. Serve sprinkled with cilantro.

Makes 9 servings

Nutrition Information: Serving Size about 1 cup, Calories 150, Total Fat 5g, Saturated Fat 1g, Protein 9g, Carbohydrate 18g, Cholesterol 12mg, Dietary Fiber 4g, Sodium 703mg

Shrimp and Pepper Bisque

- 1 bag (12 ounces) frozen bell pepper stir-fry mix, thawed
- ½ pound frozen cauliflower florets, thawed
- 1 can (14½ ounces) 99% fat-free, reduced-sodium chicken broth
- 1 stalk celery, sliced
- 1 tablespoon seafood seasoning
- ½ teaspoon dried thyme
- 12 ounces medium raw shrimp, peeled
- 2 cups fat-free half-and-half
- 2 green onions, finely chopped

Tip
For a creamier, smoother consistency, strain through several layers of damp cheesecloth.

1. Combine stir-fry mix, cauliflower, broth, celery, seafood seasoning and thyme in **CROCK-POT®** slow cooker. Cover; cook on LOW 8 hours or on HIGH 4 hours.

2. Stir in shrimp. Cover and cook 15 minutes or until shrimp are pink and opaque. Purée soup in batches in blender or food processor. Return to **CROCK-POT®** slow cooker. Stir in half-and-half. Ladle into bowls and sprinkle with green onions.

Makes 4 servings

Nutrition Information: Serving Size about 1 cup, Calories 207, Total Fat 13g, Saturated Fat 1g, Protein 23g, Carbohydrate 19g, Cholesterol 135mg, Dietary Fiber 3g, Sodium 785mg

Chilies, Soups & Stews

Thai Coconut Chicken and Rice Soup

- 1 **pound boneless, skinless chicken thighs, cut into 1-inch pieces**
- 3 **cups fat-free, reduced-sodium chicken broth**
- 1 **package (12 ounces) frozen chopped onions**
- 1 **can (4 ounces) sliced mushrooms, drained**
- 2 **tablespoons minced fresh ginger**
- 2 **tablespoons sugar**
- 1 **cup cooked long-grain rice**
- 1 **can (15 ounces) unsweetened light coconut milk**
- ½ **red bell pepper, seeded and thinly sliced**
- 3 **tablespoons chopped fresh cilantro**
- 2 **tablespoons grated lime peel**

1. Combine chicken, broth, onions, mushrooms, ginger and sugar in **CROCK-POT®** slow cooker. Cover and cook on LOW 8 to 9 hours.

2. Stir rice, coconut milk and red bell pepper into soup. Cover and cook 15 minutes longer. Turn off heat and stir in cilantro and lime peel.

Makes 8 servings

Nutrition Information: Serving Size about 1 cup, Calories 158, Total Fat 7g, Saturated Fat 4g, Protein 12g, Carbohydrate 14g, Cholesterol 46mg, Dietary Fiber 1g, Sodium 260mg

Hearty Lentil and Root Vegetable Stew

   2 **cans (about 14 ounces each) 99% fat-free chicken broth**

1½ **cups turnips, cut into 1-inch cubes**

   1 **cup dried red lentils, rinsed and sorted**

   1 **medium yellow onion, cut into ½-inch wedges**

   2 **medium carrots, cut into 1-inch pieces**

   1 **medium red bell pepper, cut into 1-inch pieces**

   ½ **teaspoon dried oregano**

   ⅛ **teaspoon red pepper flakes**

   1 **tablespoon olive oil**

   ½ **teaspoon salt**

   4 **slices bacon, crisp-cooked and crumbled**

   ½ **cup finely chopped green onions**

1. Combine broth, turnips, lentils, onion, carrots, bell pepper, oregano and pepper flakes in **CROCK-POT®** slow cooker. Stir to mix well. Cover; cook on LOW 6 hours or on HIGH 3 hours, or until lentils are tender.

2. Stir in olive oil and salt. Sprinkle each serving with bacon and green onions.

Makes 8 servings

Nutrition Information: Serving Size about 1¼ cups, Calories 152, Total Fat 4g, Saturated Fat 1g, Protein 9g, Carbohydrate 20g, Cholesterol 4mg, Dietary Fiber 5g, Sodium 679mg

Chilies, Soups & Stews

Curried Butternut Squash Soup

- **2 pounds butternut squash, rinsed, peeled, cored and chopped into 1-inch cubes**
- **1 firm crisp apple, peeled, seeded and chopped**
- **1 medium yellow onion, chopped**
- **5 cups 99% fat-free chicken broth**
- **1 tablespoon curry powder, sweet or hot**
- **¼ teaspoon ground cloves**
- **Salt and black pepper, to taste**
- **¼ cup chopped dried cranberries (optional)**

1. Place squash, apple and onion in **CROCK-POT®** slow cooker.

2. Mix together broth, curry powder and cloves in small bowl. Pour mixture into **CROCK-POT®** slow cooker. Cover; cook on LOW 5 to 5½ hours or on HIGH 4 hours, or until vegetables are tender.

3. Process soup in blender, in 2 or 3 batches, to desired consistency. Add salt and pepper. Garnish with cranberries, if desired.

Makes 8 servings

Nutrition Information: Serving Size about 1½ cups, Calories 132, Total Fat 1g, Saturated Fat 0g, Protein 4g, Carbohydrate 31g, Cholesterol 0mg, Dietary Fiber 6g, Sodium 592mg

Sweet Potato Stew

- 1 **cup chopped yellow onion**
- 1 **cup chopped celery**
- 1 **cup grated, peeled sweet potato**
- 1 **cup reduced-sodium vegetable broth**
- 2 **slices bacon, crisp-cooked and crumbled**
- 1 **cup fat-free half-and-half**
  Black pepper
- ¼ **cup minced fresh parsley**

1. Place onion, celery, sweet potato, broth and bacon in **CROCK-POT**® slow cooker. Cover; cook on LOW 6 hours or until vegetables are tender.

2. Increase heat to HIGH. Stir in half-and-half. Add water, if needed, to reach desired consistency. Cook, uncovered, 30 minutes on HIGH or until heated through.

3. Season to taste with pepper. Stir in parsley.

Makes 4 servings

Nutrition Information: Serving Size about 1¼ cups, Calories 116, Total Fat 2g, Saturated Fat 1g, Protein 5g, Carbohydrate 18g, Cholesterol 5mg, Dietary Fiber 2g, Sodium 223mg

Mushroom Barley Stew

- 1 **tablespoon olive oil**
- 1 **medium yellow onion, finely chopped**
- 1 **cup chopped carrots (about 2 carrots)**
- 1 **clove garlic, minced**
- 5 **cups reduced-sodium vegetable broth**
- 1 **cup uncooked pearl barley**
- 1 **cup dried wild mushrooms, broken into pieces**
- 1 **teaspoon salt**
- ½ **teaspoon dried thyme**
- ½ **teaspoon black pepper**

Variation

To turn this thick robust stew into a soup, add 2 to 3 additional cups of broth. Cook the same length of time.

1. Heat oil in medium skillet over medium-high heat. Add onion, carrots and garlic; cook and stir 5 minutes or until tender. Place in **CROCK-POT**® slow cooker.

2. Add broth, barley, mushrooms, salt, thyme and pepper to **CROCK-POT**® slow cooker; stir well to combine.

3. Cover; cook on LOW 6 to 7 hours. Adjust seasonings.

Makes 6 servings

Nutrition Information: Serving Size about 1½ cups, Calories 253, Total Fat 4g, Saturated Fat 1g, Protein 10g, Carbohydrate 44g, Cholesterol 0mg, Dietary Fiber 10g, Sodium 530mg

Beef, Lentil and Onion Soup

Nonstick cooking spray

¾ **pound beef for stew, cut into 1-inch pieces**

2 **cups chopped carrots**

1 **cup sliced celery**

1 **cup uncooked lentils**

2 **teaspoons dried thyme**

¼ **teaspoon black pepper**

⅛ **teaspoon salt**

3¼ **cups water**

1 **can (10½ ounces) condensed French onion soup, undiluted**

1. Spray large skillet with cooking spray. Heat skillet over medium-high heat. Add beef; cook until browned on all sides.

2. Place carrots, celery and lentils in **CROCK-POT®** slow cooker. Top with beef. Sprinkle with thyme, pepper and salt. Pour water and soup over mixture. Cover; cook on LOW 7 to 8 hours or HIGH 3½ to 4 hours or until meat and lentils are tender.

Makes 4 servings

Nutrition Information: Serving Size about 1½ cups, Calories 266, Total Fat 10g, Saturated Fat 4g, Protein 24g, Carbohydrate 21g, Cholesterol 57mg, Dietary Fiber 7g, Sodium 740mg

Chilies, Soups & Stews

Black and White Chili

1 pound chicken breasts, cut into ¾-inch pieces

1 cup coarsely chopped yellow onion

1 can (about 15 ounces) Great Northern beans, drained

1 can (about 15 ounces) 50% less sodium black beans, drained

1 can (about 14 ounces) sodium-free stewed tomatoes, undrained

2 tablespoons Texas-style chili seasoning mix

Serving Suggestion

For a change of pace, this delicious chili is excellent served over cooked rice or pasta.

1. Spray large skillet with cooking spray; heat over medium heat until hot. Add chicken and onion; cook and stir 5 minutes or until chicken is browned.

2. Combine chicken mixture, beans, tomatoes with juice and chili seasoning in **CROCK-POT®** slow cooker. Cover; cook on LOW 4 to 4½ hours.

Makes 6 servings

Nutrition Information: Serving Size about 1¼ cups, Calories 353, Total Fat 12g, Saturated Fat 3g, Protein 20g, Carbohydrate 43g, Cholesterol 31mg, Dietary Fiber 9g, Sodium 681mg

Russian Borscht

- **4** cups thinly sliced green cabbage
- **1½** pounds fresh beets, shredded
- **5** small carrots, halved lengthwise then cut into 1-inch pieces
- **1** parsnip, peeled, halved lengthwise then cut into 1-inch pieces
- **1** cup chopped onion
- **4** cloves garlic, minced
- **1** pound beef stew meat, cut into ½-inch cubes
- **1** can (about 14 ounces) diced tomatoes
- **3** cans (about 14 ounces each) 99% fat-free reduced-sodium beef broth
- **¼** cup lemon juice, or more to taste
- **1** tablespoon sugar, or more to taste
- **1** teaspoon black pepper
- Sour cream (optional)
- Fresh parsley (optional)

1. Layer ingredients in **CROCK-POT**® slow cooker in following order: cabbage, beets, carrots, parsnip, onion, garlic, beef, tomatoes, broth, lemon juice, sugar and pepper. Cover; cook on LOW 7 to 9 hours or until vegetables are crisp-tender.

2. Season with additional lemon juice and sugar, if desired. Dollop each serving with sour cream and sprinkle with parsley, if desired.

Makes 12 servings

Nutrition Information: Serving Size about 1 cup, Calories 139, Total Fat 4g, Saturated Fat 1g, Protein 11g, Carbohydrate 15g, Cholesterol 24mg, Dietary Fiber 4g, Sodium 345mg

Chilies, Soups & Stews

Chicken and Chile Pepper Stew

1 **pound boneless, skinless chicken thighs, cut into ½-inch pieces**

1 **pound small potatoes, cut lengthwise into halves, then crosswise into slices**

1 **cup chopped yellow onion**

2 **poblano peppers, seeded and cut into ½-inch pieces***

1 **jalapeño pepper, seeded and finely chopped***

3 **cloves garlic, minced**

3 **cups fat-free, reduced-sodium chicken broth**

1 **can (14 ounces) no-salt-added diced tomatoes, undrained**

2 **tablespoons chili powder**

1 **teaspoon dried oregano**

Hot peppers can sting and irritate the skin, so wear rubber gloves when handling peppers and do not touch your eyes.

1. Place chicken, potatoes, onion, poblano peppers, jalapeño pepper and garlic in **CROCK-POT®** slow cooker.

2. Stir together broth, tomatoes with juice, chili powder and oregano in large bowl. Pour into **CROCK-POT®** slow cooker. Stir well to blend. Cover; cook on LOW 8 to 9 hours.

Makes 6 servings

Nutrition Information: Serving Size about 1¼ cups, Calories 192, Total Fat 6g, Saturated Fat 2g, Protein 18g, Carbohydrate 22g, Cholesterol 61mg, Dietary Fiber 4g, Sodium 310mg

Black Bean and Turkey Stew

   3 **cans (15 ounces each) 50% less sodium black beans, rinsed and drained**

1½ **cups chopped yellow onions**

1½ **cups fat-free, reduced-sodium chicken broth**

   1 **cup sliced celery**

   1 **cup chopped red bell pepper**

   4 **cloves garlic, minced**

1½ **teaspoons dried oregano leaves**

   ¾ **teaspoon ground coriander**

   ½ **teaspoon ground cumin**

   ¼ **teaspoon ground red pepper**

   6 **ounces cooked turkey sausage, thinly sliced**

1. Combine all ingredients except sausage in **CROCK-POT®** slow cooker. Cover; cook on LOW 6 to 8 hours.

2. Transfer about 1½ cups bean mixture from **CROCK-POT®** slow cooker to blender or food processor; purée bean mixture. Return to **CROCK-POT®** slow cooker. Stir in sausage. Cover; cook on LOW an additional 10 to 15 minutes.

Makes 6 servings

Nutrition Information: Serving Size about 1½ cups, Calories 193, Total Fat 3g, Saturated Fat 1g, Protein 15g, Carbohydrate 35g, Cholesterol 21mg, Dietary Fiber 12g, Sodium 732mg

Butternut Squash-Apple Soup

3 packages (12 ounces each) frozen cooked winter squash, thawed and drained **or** about 4½ cups mashed cooked butternut squash

2 cans (about 14 ounces each) 99% fat-free chicken broth

1 medium Golden Delicious apple, peeled, cored and chopped

2 tablespoons minced yellow onion

1 tablespoon packed brown sugar

1 teaspoon minced fresh sage **or** ½ teaspoon ground sage

¼ teaspoon ground ginger

½ cup whipping cream **or** half-and-half

Tip
For thicker soup, use only 3 cups chicken broth.

1. Combine squash, broth, apple, onion, brown sugar, sage and ginger in **CROCK-POT®** slow cooker.

2. Cover; cook on LOW 6 hours or on HIGH 3 hours or until squash is tender.

3. Purée soup in food processor or blender. Stir in cream just before serving.

Makes 8 servings

Nutrition Information: Serving Size about 1½ cups, Calories 112, Total Fat 2g, Saturated Fat 1g, Protein 3g, Carbohydrate 25g, Cholesterol 6mg, Dietary Fiber 6g, Sodium 413mg

Vegetarian Chili

- 1 **tablespoon vegetable oil**
- 1 **cup chopped yellow onion**
- 1 **cup chopped red bell pepper**
- 2 **tablespoons minced jalapeño pepper***
- 1 **clove garlic, minced**
- 1 **can (28 ounces) sodium-free stewed tomatoes, crushed**
- 1 **can (15 ounces) black beans, rinsed and drained**
- 1 **can (15 ounces) chickpeas, rinsed and drained**
- ½ **cup frozen corn kernels, thawed and drained**
- ¼ **cup tomato paste**
- 1 **teaspoon sugar**
- 1 **teaspoon ground cumin**
- 1 **teaspoon dried basil**
- 1 **teaspoon chili powder**
- ¼ **teaspoon black pepper**
- **Sour cream and shredded Cheddar cheese (optional)**

Jalapeño peppers can sting and irritate the skin, so wear rubber gloves when handling peppers and do not touch your eyes.

1. Heat oil in large skillet over medium-high heat until hot. Add onion, bell pepper, jalapeño pepper and garlic; cook and stir 5 minutes or until vegetables are tender. Transfer vegetables to **CROCK-POT®** slow cooker.

2. Add remaining ingredients except sour cream and cheese; mix well. Cover; cook on LOW 4 to 5 hours.

3. Garnish with sour cream and cheese, if desired.

Makes 4 servings

Nutrition Information: Serving Size about 1½ cups, Calories 329, Total Fat 6g, Saturated Fat 0g, Protein 15g, Carbohydrate 57g, Cholesterol 0mg, Dietary Fiber 14g, Sodium 858mg

Chilies, Soups & Stews

Savory Pea Soup with Sausage

- **8** ounces smoked sausage, cut lengthwise into halves, then cut into ½-inch pieces
- **1** package (16 ounces) dried split peas, rinsed and sorted
- **3** medium carrots, sliced
- **2** stalks celery, sliced
- **1** medium yellow onion, chopped
- **¾** teaspoon dried marjoram leaves
- **1** bay leaf
- **2** cans (14½ ounces each) reduced-sodium chicken broth

1. Heat medium nonstick skillet over medium heat. Add sausage; cook 5 to 8 minutes or until browned. Drain fat. Combine sausage, peas, carrots, celery, onion, marjoram and bay leaf in **CROCK-POT**® slow cooker. Pour broth over mixture.

2. Cover; cook on LOW 4 to 5 hours or until peas are tender. Remove and discard bay leaf. Cover; let stand 15 minutes to thicken.

Makes 6 servings

Nutrition Information: Serving Size about 1¼ cups, Calories 411, Total Fat 12g, Saturated Fat 4g, Protein 26g, Carbohydrate 52g, Cholesterol 22mg, Dietary Fiber 21g, Sodium 705mg

Lentil and Portobello Soup

- 2 **portobello mushrooms (about 8 ounces total), cleaned and trimmed**
- 1 **tablespoon olive oil**
- 1 **medium yellow onion, chopped**
- 2 **medium carrots, cut into ½-inch-thick rounds**
- 2 **cloves garlic, minced**
- 1 **cup dried lentils**
- 1 **can (28 ounces) diced tomatoes in juice, undrained**
- 1 **can (14½ ounces) vegetable broth**
- 1 **teaspoon dried rosemary**
- 1 **bay leaf**
  Salt
  Black pepper

1. Remove stems from mushrooms; coarsely chop stems. Cut each cap in half, then cut each half into ½-inch pieces. Set aside.

2. Heat oil in large skillet over medium heat. Add onion, carrots and garlic and cook, stirring occasionally, until onion softens. Transfer to **CROCK-POT**® slow cooker. Layer lentils, tomatoes with juice, vegetable broth, mushrooms caps and stems, dried rosemary and bay leaf on top of carrots and onion. Cover; cook on HIGH 5 to 6 hours or until lentils are tender. Remove bay leaf and season to taste with salt and pepper before serving. Serve hot.

Makes 6 servings

Nutrition Information: Serving Size about 1½ cups, Calories 185, Total Fat 3g, Saturated Fat 1g, Protein 10g, Carbohydrate 31g, Cholesterol 0mg, Dietary Fiber 11g, Sodium 654mg

Beef Main Dishes

Ginger Beef with Peppers and Mushrooms

- 1½ pounds beef top round steak for London broil, cut into ¾-inch cubes
- 24 baby carrots
- 1 red bell pepper, seeded and chopped
- 1 green bell pepper, seeded and chopped
- 1 medium yellow onion, chopped
- 1 package (8 ounces) fresh mushrooms, cut in halves
- 2 tablespoons grated fresh ginger
- 1 cup 99% fat-free, reduced-sodium beef broth
- ½ cup hoisin sauce
- ¼ cup quick-cooking tapioca

  Hot cooked white rice (optional)

Combine all ingredients except cooked rice in **CROCK-POT**® slow cooker. Cover and cook on LOW 8 to 9 hours. Serve over white rice, if desired.

Makes 6 servings

Nutrition Information: Serving Size about 1 cup, Calories 349, Total Fat 11g, Saturated Fat 4g, Protein 38g, Carbohydrate 25g, Cholesterol 66mg, Dietary Fiber 3g, Sodium 502mg

Beef Main Dishes

Beef Chile Sauce

- **2 tablespoons vegetable oil**
- **2 pounds lean beef round roast, cut into bite-size pieces**
- **1 medium yellow onion, peeled and finely chopped**
- **2 cloves garlic, diced**
- **1¾ cups water**
- **5 canned whole green chiles, peeled and diced***
- **1 canned chipotle pepper in adobo sauce, diced****
- **1 teaspoon salt**
- **1 teaspoon all-purpose flour**
- **1 teaspoon dried oregano**
- **½ teaspoon ground cumin**
- **¼ teaspoon black pepper**
- **Prepared polenta (optional)**
- **Fresh cilantro (optional)**

Green chiles can sting and irritate the skin, so wear rubber gloves when handling peppers and do not touch your eyes.

**Chipotle peppers can sting and irritate the skin, so wear rubber gloves when handling peppers and do not touch your eyes.*

1. Heat oil in large skillet over medium heat until hot. Sear beef on all sides, turning as it browns. Add onion and garlic during last few minutes of searing. Transfer to **CROCK-POT®** slow cooker.

2. Add water, chiles and chipotle pepper. Stir well to combine. Cover; cook on LOW 2 hours.

3. Combine salt, flour, oregano, cumin and black pepper in a small bowl. Add to **CROCK-POT®** slow cooker. Stir well to combine. Cover; cook on LOW 3 to 4 hours longer. To serve over polenta, if desired, slice polenta into ½-inch-thick pieces. Place on greased baking sheet. Broil until crispy, about 4 minutes on each side. Transfer polenta to individual plates and spoon meat and sauce over it. Garnish with fresh cilantro, if desired.

Makes 6 servings

Nutrition Information: Serving Size about 1¼ cups, Calories 251, Total Fat 11g, Saturated Fat 3g, Protein 34g, Carbohydrate 4g, Cholesterol 88mg, Dietary Fiber 1g, Sodium 527mg

Hearty Beef Short Ribs

1½ pounds flanken-style beef short ribs, bone-in

¾ tablespoon coarse salt

1 tablespoon black pepper

1 tablespoon olive oil, divided

2 carrots, cut into ¼-inch dice

2 celery stalks, cut into ¼-inch dice

1 large yellow onion, cut into ¼-inch dice

3 cloves garlic, minced

3 bay leaves

⅓ cup red wine

⅓ cup crushed tomatoes

⅓ cup balsamic vinegar

Tip

For a change of pace from ordinary short rib recipes, ask your butcher for flanken-style beef short ribs. Flanken-style ribs are cut across the bones into wide, flat portions. They provide all the meaty flavor of the more common English-style short ribs with smaller, more manageable bones.

1. Season ribs with salt and black pepper. Heat oil in large skillet. Cook ribs until just browned, about 2 to 3 minutes per side. Transfer ribs to **CROCK-POT®** slow cooker. Add carrots, celery, onion, garlic and bay leaves.

2. Combine wine, tomatoes and vinegar in small bowl. Season with salt and black pepper, if desired. Pour mixture into **CROCK-POT®** slow cooker. Cover; cook on LOW 8 to 9 hours or on HIGH 5½ to 6 hours, turning once or twice, until meat is tender and falling off the bone.

3. Remove ribs from **CROCK-POT®** slow cooker. Process sauce in blender to desired consistency. To serve, pour sauce over ribs.

Makes 8 servings

Nutrition Information: Serving Size ⅛ ribs and about ¼ cup sauce, Calories 202, Total Fat 11g, Saturated Fat 4g, Protein 17g, Carbohydrate 7g, Cholesterol 50mg, Dietary Fiber 1g, Sodium 632mg

Beef Main Dishes

Asian Beef with Mandarin Oranges

- 2 **tablespoons vegetable oil**
- 2 **pounds lean boneless beef chuck, cut into ½-inch strips**
- 1 **small yellow onion, thinly sliced**
- ⅓ **cup reduced-sodium soy sauce**
- ¼ **teaspoon salt**
- 2 **teaspoons minced fresh ginger**
- 1 **small green bell pepper, sliced**
- 1 **package (about 3 ounces) shiitake mushrooms, sliced**
- 1 **head (about 5 ounces) bok choy, cleaned and chopped**
- 1 **can (5 ounces) sliced water chestnuts, drained**
- 2 **tablespoons cornstarch**
- 1 **can (11 ounces) mandarin oranges in light syrup, drained, syrup reserved**
- 2 **cups 99% fat-free beef broth**
- 6 **cups steamed rice**

1. Heat vegetable oil over medium-high heat. Add beef, in batches if necessary, and cook, turning to brown all sides. Transfer beef to **CROCK-POT®** slow cooker as it is browned.

2. Add onion to same skillet. Stir over medium heat until softened. Next, add soy sauce, salt, ginger, green pepper, mushrooms, bok choy and water chestnuts, and cook until bok choy is wilted, about 5 minutes. Spoon mixture over beef.

3. Whisk together cornstarch and reserved mandarin orange syrup in medium bowl. Stir in beef broth and pour over ingredients in **CROCK-POT®** slow cooker. Cover and cook on LOW 10 hours or on HIGH 5 to 6 hours, or until beef is tender.

4. Stir in mandarin oranges. Spoon steamed rice into shallow serving bowl and spoon beef over rice.

Makes 6 servings

Nutrition Information: Serving Size about 1½ cups, Calories 409, Total Fat 12g, Saturated Fat 3g, Protein 29g, Carbohydrate 47g, Cholesterol 65mg, Dietary Fiber 2g, Sodium 717mg

Braised Chipotle Beef

      3 **pounds lean chuck roast, cut into 2-inch pieces**
      2 **tablespoons vegetable oil, divided**
      1 **large yellow onion, cut into 1-inch pieces**
      2 **red bell peppers, seeded and cut into 1-inch pieces**
      1 **tablespoon minced garlic**
      1 **tablespoon chipotle chili powder***
      1 **tablespoon paprika**
      1 **teaspoon dried oregano**
      1 **tablespoon ground cumin**
      3 **tablespoons tomato paste**
   1½ **teaspoons salt**
      ½ **teaspoon ground black pepper**
      1 **cup 99% fat-free beef broth**
      1 **can (about 14 ounces) diced tomatoes, drained**
        Hot cooked rice (optional)

Or substitute conventional chili powder.

1. Pat beef dry with paper towels. Heat 1 tablespoon oil in large skillet over medium-high heat. Working in batches, cook beef in skillet, turning to brown all sides. Transfer each batch to **CROCK-POT®** slow cooker as it is finished.

2. Return skillet to medium heat. Add remaining tablespoon oil. Add onion and cook, stirring occasionally, until just softened. Add bell peppers and cook 2 minutes. Stir in garlic, chili powder, paprika, oregano, cumin, tomato paste, salt and black pepper. Cook and stir 1 minute. Transfer to **CROCK-POT®** slow cooker.

3. Return skillet to heat and add beef broth. Cook, stirring to scrape up any browned bits. Pour over beef in **CROCK-POT®** slow cooker. Stir in tomatoes. Cover and cook on LOW 7 hours or until beef is tender. Skim fat from sauce. Serve over hot cooked rice, if desired.

Makes 8 servings

Nutrition Information: Serving Size about 1 cup, Calories 306, Total Fat 11g, Saturated Fat 3g, Protein 40g, Carbohydrate 9g, Cholesterol 75mg, Dietary Fiber 2g, Sodium 789mg

Beef Main Dishes

Meatballs and Spaghetti Sauce

Meatballs

- 2 pounds 95% lean ground beef
- 1 cup bread crumbs
- 1 medium yellow onion, chopped
- 2 eggs, beaten
- ¼ cup minced flat-leaf parsley
- 2 teaspoons minced garlic
- ½ teaspoon dry mustard
- ½ teaspoon black pepper
  Olive oil

Spaghetti Sauce

- 1 can (28 ounces) peeled whole tomatoes
- ½ cup chopped fresh basil
- 2 tablespoons olive oil
- 2 cloves garlic, or to taste, finely minced
- 1 teaspoon sugar
  Salt and black pepper, to taste

  Cooked spaghetti

1. Combine all meatball ingredients except oil. Form into walnut-sized balls. Heat oil in skillet over medium heat until hot. Sear meatballs on all sides, turning as they brown. Transfer to **CROCK-POT**® slow cooker.

2. Combine all sauce ingredients in medium bowl. Pour over meatballs, stirring to coat. Cover; cook on LOW 3 to 5 hours or on HIGH 2 to 4 hours.

3. Adjust seasonings, if desired. Serve over spaghetti.

Makes 8 servings

Nutrition Information: Serving Size about 1 cup, Calories 291, Total Fat 11g, Saturated Fat 4g, Protein 29g, Carbohydrate 16g, Cholesterol 124mg, Dietary Fiber 2g, Sodium 372mg

Asian Ginger Beef over Bok Choy

  2 tablespoons peanut oil

1½ pounds boneless beef chuck roast, cut into 1-inch pieces

  3 green onions, cut into ½-inch slices

  6 cloves garlic

  1 cup 99% fat-free, reduced-sodium chicken broth

  ½ cup water

  ¼ cup reduced-sodium soy sauce

  2 teaspoons ground ginger

  1 teaspoon Asian chili paste

  9 ounces fresh udon noodles or vermicelli, cooked and drained

  9 ounces bok choy, trimmed, washed and cut into 1-inch pieces

  ½ cup minced fresh cilantro

1. Heat oil in large skillet over medium-high heat until hot. Sear beef on all sides in batches to prevent crowding, turning each piece as it browns. Sear last batch of beef with onions and garlic.

2. Transfer to **CROCK-POT**® slow cooker. Add broth, water, soy sauce, ginger and chili paste. Stir well to combine. Cover; cook on LOW 7 to 8 hours or on HIGH 3 to 4 hours, or until beef is very tender.

3. Just before serving, turn **CROCK-POT**® slow cooker to HIGH. Add noodles to **CROCK-POT**® slow cooker and stir well. Add bok choy and stir again. Cook on HIGH until bok choy is tender-crisp, about 15 minutes.

4. Garnish beef with cilantro and serve while hot.

Makes 8 servings

Nutrition Information: Serving Size about 1½ cups, Calories 295, Total Fat 10g, Saturated Fat 3g, Protein 24g, Carbohydrate 26g, Cholesterol 49mg, Dietary Fiber 3g, Sodium 488mg

Beef Main Dishes

Yankee Pot Roast and Vegetables

2½ **pounds beef chuck pot roast**

Salt and black pepper

3 **unpeeled medium baking potatoes (about 1 pound), cut into quarters**

2 **large carrots, cut into ¾-inch slices**

2 **stalks celery, cut into ¾-inch slices**

1 **medium yellow onion, sliced**

1 **large parsnip, cut into ¾-inch slices**

2 **bay leaves**

1 **teaspoon dried rosemary**

½ **teaspoon dried thyme**

½ **cup 99% fat-free, reduced-sodium beef broth**

Tip

To make gravy, ladle cooking liquid into 2-cup measure; let stand 5 minutes. Skim off fat and discard. Measure remaining cooking liquid and heat to a boil in small saucepan. For each cup of cooking liquid, mix 2 tablespoons flour with ¼ cup cold water until smooth. Stir flour mixture into boiling cooking liquid, stirring constantly 1 minute or until thickened.

1. Trim excess fat from beef and discard. Cut beef into serving-size pieces; sprinkle with salt and pepper.

2. Combine potatoes, carrots, celery, onion, parsnip, bay leaves, rosemary and thyme in **CROCK-POT**® slow cooker. Place beef over vegetables. Pour broth over beef. Cover; cook on LOW 8½ to 9 hours, or until beef is fork-tender.

3. Transfer beef to serving platter. Arrange vegetables around beef. Remove and discard bay leaves before serving.

Makes 12 servings

Nutrition Information: Serving Size about 1¼ cups, Calories 182, Total Fat 4g, Saturated Fat 2g, Protein 22g, Carbohydrate 13g, Cholesterol 42mg, Dietary Fiber 3g, Sodium 110mg

Beef Main Dishes

Swiss Steak Stew

- **4 pounds boneless beef top sirloin steaks (2 or 3 steaks)**
- **2 cans (about 14 ounces each) diced tomatoes, undrained**
- **2 medium green bell peppers, cut into ½-inch strips**
- **2 medium yellow onions, chopped**
- **1 tablespoon seasoned salt**
- **1 teaspoon black pepper**

Cut each steak into 3 to 4 pieces; place in **CROCK-POT®** slow cooker. Add tomatoes with juice, bell peppers and onions. Season with salt and black pepper. Cover; cook on LOW 8 hours or until meat is tender.

Makes 10 servings

Nutrition Information: Serving Size about 1¼ cups, Calories 267, Total Fat 7g, Saturated Fat 3g, Protein 42g, Carbohydrate 7g, Cholesterol 97mg, Dietary Fiber 1g, Sodium 746mg

Easy Beef Stroganoff

- **1½ pounds well-trimmed beef top round steak, cut into 1-inch cubes**
- **4 medium potatoes, cut into 1-inch cubes**
- **4 carrots, cut into 1½-inch pieces or 4 cups baby carrots**
- **1 medium yellow onion, cut into 8 wedges**
- **2 cans (8 ounces each) tomato sauce**
- **1 teaspoon salt**
- **½ teaspoon black pepper**
- **Hot cooked egg noodles**
- **Chopped parsley**

Combine all ingredients except noodles and parsley in **CROCK-POT®** slow cooker. Cover; cook on LOW 8 to 10 hours or until vegetables are tender. Serve over hot cooked egg noodles; garnish with parsley, as desired.

Makes 8 servings

Nutrition Information: Serving Size about 1 cup, Calories 255, Total Fat 9g, Saturated Fat 3g, Protein 20g, Carbohydrate 24g, Cholesterol 54mg, Dietary Fiber 4g, Sodium 681mg

Swiss Steak Stew

Beef Main Dishes

Burgundy and Wild Cremini Mushroom Pilaf

- 2 **tablespoons vegetable oil**
- 2 **cups uncooked converted long-grain white rice**
- 1 **medium yellow onion, chopped**
- 1 **cup sliced wild cremini mushrooms**
- 1 **small zucchini, thinly sliced**
- 3½ **cups 99% fat-free beef broth**
- ½ **cup burgundy or other red wine**
- ½ **teaspoon salt**
- ¼ **teaspoon black pepper**
- 4 **tablespoons (½ stick) unsalted butter, melted**

1. Heat oil in skillet over medium heat until hot. Add rice, onion, mushrooms and zucchini. Cook and stir 4 to 5 minutes until rice is slightly browned and onion is soft. Transfer to **CROCK-POT®** slow cooker.

2. Add broth, burgundy, salt and pepper. Drizzle melted butter over all. Stir once. Cover; cook on LOW 6 to 8 hours.

Makes 6 servings

Nutrition Information: Serving Size about 1¼ cups, Calories 355, Total Fat 11g, Saturated Fat 4g, Protein 6g, Carbohydrate 53g, Cholesterol 15mg, Dietary Fiber 1g, Sodium 720mg

Middle Eastern Beef and Eggplant Stew

- 1 teaspoon olive oil
- 1 small eggplant, trimmed and cut into 1-inch chunks
- 2 cups shiitake or cremini mushrooms, quartered
- 1 can (about 14 ounces) no-salt-added diced tomatoes
- ½ pound beef top round steak, cut into 1-inch pieces*
- 1 medium yellow onion, chopped
- 1 cup 99% fat-free, reduced-sodium beef broth
- 1 clove garlic, minced
- ½ teaspoon salt
- ⅓ teaspoon ground cumin
- ¼ teaspoon red pepper flakes
- ¼ teaspoon ground cinnamon
- 2 teaspoons grated lemon peel
- ⅛ teaspoon black pepper

Steak should be trimmed of fat before weighing to yield 8 ounces of very lean beef.

1. Heat oil in large nonstick skillet over medium-high heat. Add eggplant and cook 3 to 5 minutes, stirring frequently or until lightly browned on all sides. Transfer to **CROCK-POT®** slow cooker.

2. Stir in remaining ingredients. Cover; cook on LOW 6 hours.

Makes 4 servings

Nutrition Information: Serving Size about 1¼ cups, Calories 183, Total Fat 6g, Saturated Fat 2g, Protein 17g, Carbohydrate 16g, Cholesterol 23mg, Dietary Fiber 6g, Sodium 455mg

Beef Main Dishes

Barley Beef Stroganoff

⅔ cup uncooked pearl barley (not quick-cooking)

2½ cups water

1 package (6 ounces) sliced mushrooms

½ teaspoon dried marjoram

½ pound 95% lean ground beef

½ cup chopped celery

½ cup minced green onions

½ teaspoon black pepper

¼ cup fat-free half-and-half

Minced fresh parsley (optional)

Tip

Browning ground beef before adding it to the **CROCK-POT®** slow cooker helps reduce the fat. Just remember to drain off the fat in the skillet before transferring the meat to the **CROCK-POT®** slow cooker.

1. Place barley, water, mushrooms and marjoram in **CROCK-POT®** slow cooker. Cover; cook on LOW 6 to 7 hours.

2. Cook and stir ground beef in large nonstick skillet over medium heat until browned and crumbly, about 7 minutes. Drain and discard fat. Add celery, green onions and pepper; cook and stir 3 minutes. Transfer to **CROCK-POT®** slow cooker.

3. Mix in half-and-half. Cover; cook on HIGH 10 to 15 minutes, until beef is hot and vegetables are tender. Garnish with parsley, if desired.

Makes 6 servings

Nutrition Information: Serving Size about 1¼ cups, Calories 160, Total Fat 3g, Saturated Fat 1g, Protein 14g, Carbohydrate 20g, Cholesterol 28mg, Dietary Fiber 4g, Sodium 45mg

Asian Short Ribs

- ½ **cup 99% fat-free, reduced-sodium beef broth**
- ¼ **cup reduced-sodium soy sauce**
- ¼ **cup dry sherry**
- 1 **tablespoon honey**
- 1 **tablespoon grated fresh ginger***
- 2 **teaspoons minced garlic**
- 2 **pounds boneless beef short ribs**
- 1 **teaspoon salt**
- ½ **teaspoon black pepper**
- ½ **cup chopped green onions (optional)**
- **Hot cooked rice**

To mince ginger quickly, cut a small chunk, remove the skin and put through a garlic press. Store remaining unpeeled ginger in a plastic food storage bag in the refrigerator for up to 3 weeks.

1. Stir together beef broth, soy sauce, sherry, honey, ginger and garlic in **CROCK-POT®** slow cooker.

2. Season short ribs with salt and pepper. Coat large skillet with nonstick cooking spray and place over medium-high heat. Working in batches, cook beef in skillet, turning to brown all sides. Transfer each batch to **CROCK-POT®** slow cooker as it is finished, turning to coat all sides with sauce.

3. Cover and cook on LOW 7 to 8 hours or until meat is fork-tender.

4. Remove beef and place on serving dish. Garnish with green onions, if desired. Serve with cooked rice.

Makes 6 servings

Nutrition Information: Serving Size about 1¼ cups, Calories 219, Total Fat 12g, Saturated Fat 4g, Protein 22g, Carbohydrate 3g, Cholesterol 67mg, Dietary Fiber 0g, Sodium 660mg

Beef Main Dishes

Beef Roast with Dark Rum Sauce

- 1 teaspoon ground allspice
- ½ teaspoon salt
- ½ teaspoon black pepper
- ¼ teaspoon ground cloves
- 3 pounds lean beef bottom round roast
- 2 tablespoons extra-virgin olive oil
- 1 cup dark rum, divided
- ½ cup 99% fat-free beef broth
- 2 cloves garlic, minced
- 2 whole bay leaves, broken in half
- ½ cup packed dark brown sugar
- ¼ cup lime juice

Tip

To ensure even cooking, cut roasts into 2 or 3 equal-size pieces small enough to fit in a single layer in your **CROCK-POT®** slow cooker.

1. In a small bowl, combine allspice, salt, pepper and cloves. Rub spices onto all sides of roast.

2. Heat oil in skillet over medium heat until hot. Sear beef on all sides, turning as it browns. Transfer to **CROCK-POT®** slow cooker. Add ½ cup rum, broth, garlic and bay leaves. Cover; cook on LOW 1 hour.

3. In a small bowl, combine remaining ½ cup rum, brown sugar and lime juice, stirring well. Pour over roast. Continue cooking on LOW 4 to 6 hours, or until beef is fork-tender. Baste beef occasionally with sauce.

4. Remove and slice roast. Spoon sauce over beef to serve.

Makes 6 servings

Nutrition Information: Serving Size about 1¼ cups, Calories 467 Total Fat 12g, Saturated Fat 4g, Protein 51g, Carbohydrate 20g, Cholesterol 132mg, Dietary Fiber 0g, Sodium 408mg

Middle Eastern-Spiced Beef, Tomatoes and Beans

1   **tablespoon extra-virgin olive oil, divided**

1½ **pounds lean boneless beef chuck roast, cut into 1-inch pieces, divided**

1   **can (14½ ounces) no-salt-added diced tomatoes, undrained**

6   **ounces fresh green beans, trimmed and broken into 1-inch pieces**

1   **cup chopped yellow onion**

½   **teaspoon ground cinnamon**

¼   **teaspoon ground allspice**

1½ **teaspoons sugar**

¼   **teaspoon garlic powder**

½   **teaspoon salt, or to taste**

¼   **teaspoon black pepper**

    Hot cooked couscous or rice (optional)

1. Heat 2 teaspoons oil in large skillet over medium-high heat. Add half of beef cubes and cook, stirring frequently, until browned on all sides. Transfer to **CROCK-POT®** slow cooker. Add remaining oil and repeat with remaining beef.

2. Stir in tomatoes with juice, beans, onion, cinnamon, allspice, sugar and garlic powder. Cover and cook on LOW 8 hours or on HIGH 4 hours.

3. Stir in salt and pepper and let stand uncovered 15 minutes to allow flavors to absorb and thicken slightly. Serve as is or over cooked couscous or rice, if desired.

Makes about 4 servings

Nutrition Information: Serving Size about 1¼ cups, Calories 326, Total Fat 12g, Saturated Fat 4g, Protein 39g, Carbohydrate 14g, Cholesterol 85mg, Dietary Fiber 3g, Sodium 418mg

Beef Main Dishes

Korean Barbecue Beef

  2 **pounds beef short ribs**

  ¼ **cup chopped green onions (white and green parts)**

  ¼ **cup soy sauce**

  ¼ **cup water**

  1 **tablespoon packed brown sugar**

  2 **teaspoons minced fresh ginger**

  2 **teaspoons minced garlic**

  ½ **teaspoon black pepper**

      Dark sesame oil, to taste

      Hot cooked rice or linguine pasta (optional)

  2 **teaspoons sesame seeds, toasted (optional)**

Tip
Three pounds of boneless short ribs can be substituted for the beef short ribs.

1. Place ribs in **CROCK-POT®** slow cooker. Combine green onions, soy sauce, water, brown sugar, ginger, garlic and pepper in medium bowl; mix well and pour over ribs. Cover; cook on LOW 7 to 8 hours or until ribs are fork-tender.

2. Remove ribs from cooking liquid. Cool slightly. Trim excess fat and discard. Cut rib meat into bite-size pieces, discarding bones and fat.

3. Let cooking liquid stand 5 minutes to allow fat to rise. Skim off fat and discard. Stir sesame oil into cooking liquid. Return beef to **CROCK-POT®** slow cooker. Cover; cook on LOW 15 to 30 minutes or until hot. Serve over rice, garnished with sesame seeds, if desired.

Makes 8 servings

Nutrition Information: Serving Size about 1 cup, Calories 214, Total Fat 12g, Saturated Fat 4g, Protein 22g, Carbohydrate 3g, Cholesterol 67mg, Dietary Fiber 0g, Sodium 732mg

Sauvignon Blanc Beef with Beets and Thyme

- 1 pound red or yellow beets, scrubbed and quartered
- 1 tablespoon extra-virgin olive oil
- 3 pounds lean beef chuck roast
- 1 medium yellow onion, peeled and quartered
- 2 cloves garlic, minced
- 5 sprigs fresh thyme
- 1 whole bay leaf
- 2 whole cloves
- 1 cup 99% fat-free chicken broth
- 1 cup Sauvignon Blanc or other white wine
- 2 tablespoons tomato paste
- Salt and black pepper, to taste

1. Layer beets evenly in **CROCK-POT®** slow cooker.

2. Heat oil in large skillet over medium heat until hot. Sear roast on all sides 4 to 5 minutes, turning as it browns. Add onion and garlic during last few minutes of searing. Transfer to **CROCK-POT®** slow cooker.

3. Add thyme, bay leaf and cloves. Combine broth, wine and tomato paste in medium bowl. Add salt and pepper. Mix well to combine. Pour over roast and beets. Cover; cook on LOW 8 to 10 hours, or until roast is fork-tender and beets are tender.

Makes 6 servings

Nutrition Information: Serving Size about 1¼ cups, Calories 400, Total Fat 12g, Saturated Fat 4g, Protein 52g, Carbohydrate 11g, Cholesterol 100mg, Dietary Fiber 3g, Sodium 386mg

Beef Main Dishes

Best Beef Brisket Sandwich Ever

1   well-trimmed, lean beef brisket (about 3 pounds)
2   cups apple cider, divided
1   head garlic, cloves separated, crushed and peeled
2   tablespoons whole peppercorns
⅓   cup chopped fresh thyme **or 2 tablespoons dried thyme**
1   tablespoon mustard seeds
1   tablespoon Cajun seasoning
1   teaspoon ground allspice
1   teaspoon ground cumin
1   teaspoon celery seeds
2 to 4 whole cloves
1   bottle (12 ounces) dark beer
12   sourdough sandwich rolls, sliced in half

Tip

Unless you have a 5-, 6- or 7-quart **CROCK-POT®** slow cooker, cut any roast larger than 2½ pounds in half so it cooks completely.

1. Place brisket, ½ cup cider, garlic, peppercorns, thyme, mustard seeds, Cajun seasoning, allspice, cumin, celery seeds and cloves in large resealable food storage bag. Seal bag; marinate in refrigerator overnight.

2. Place brisket and marinade in **CROCK-POT®** slow cooker. Add remaining 1½ cups apple cider and beer. Cover; cook on LOW 10 hours or until brisket is tender.

3. Strain sauce; drizzle over meat. Slice brisket and place on sandwich rolls.

Makes 12 servings

Nutrition Information: Serving Size 1 sandwich, Calories 331, Total Fat 5g, Saturated Fat 2g, Protein 30g, Carbohydrate 36g, Cholesterol 46mg, Dietary Fiber 2g, Sodium 558mg

Beef Bourguignonne

- **3 pounds boneless beef top sirloin steak, trimmed of fat**
- **½ cup all-purpose flour**
- **4 slices bacon, diced**
- **2 medium carrots, diced**
- **8 small red potatoes, unpeeled, cut into quarters**
- **8 fresh mushrooms, sliced**
- **20 pearl onions**
- **3 cloves garlic, minced**
- **1 bay leaf**
- **1 teaspoon dried marjoram leaves**
- **½ teaspoon dried thyme leaves**
- **½ teaspoon salt**
- **Black pepper, to taste**
- **2½ cups reduced-sodium beef broth**

1. Cut beef into 1-inch pieces. Coat with flour, shaking off excess; set aside. Cook bacon in large skillet over medium heat until partially cooked. Add beef; brown on all sides. Drain and discard fat.

2. Layer carrots, potatoes, mushrooms, onions, garlic, bay leaf, marjoram, thyme, salt, pepper, to taste, and beef mixture in **CROCK-POT®** slow cooker. Pour broth over all.

3. Cover; cook on LOW 8 to 9 hours or until beef is tender. Remove and discard bay leaf before serving.

Makes 10 servings

Nutrition Information: Serving Size about 1¼ cups, Calories 367, Total Fat 10g, Saturated Fat 4g, Protein 36g, Carbohydrate 32g, Cholesterol 80mg, Dietary Fiber 3g, Sodium 483mg

Beef Main Dishes

Beef with Green Chiles

- ¼ **cup plus 1 tablespoon all-purpose flour, divided**
- ½ **teaspoon salt**
- ¼ **teaspoon black pepper**
- 1 **pound beef stew meat**
- 1 **tablespoon vegetable oil**
- 2 **cloves garlic, minced**
- 1 **cup 99% fat-free, reduced-sodium beef broth**
- 1 **can (7 ounces) diced mild green chiles, drained**
- ½ **teaspoon dried oregano**
- 2 **tablespoons water**
  - **Hot cooked rice (optional)**
  - **Diced tomato (optional)**

Tip
Use 2 cans of chiles for a slightly hotter taste.

1. Combine ¼ cup flour, salt and pepper in resealable food storage bag. Add beef; shake to coat beef. Heat oil in large skillet over medium-high heat. Add beef and garlic. Brown beef on all sides. Place beef mixture into **CROCK-POT**® slow cooker. Add broth to skillet scraping up any browned bits. Pour broth mixture into **CROCK-POT**® slow cooker. Add green chiles and oregano.

2. Cover; cook on LOW 7 to 8 hours. For thicker sauce, combine remaining 1 tablespoon flour and water in small bowl stirring until mixture is smooth. Stir mixture into **CROCK-POT**® slow cooker; mix well. Cover and cook until thickened.

3. Serve with rice and garnish with diced tomato, if desired.

Makes 4 servings

Nutrition Information: Serving Size about 1¼ cups, Calories 234, Total Fat 8g, Saturated Fat 2g, Protein 27g, Carbohydrate 11g, Cholesterol 50mg, Dietary Fiber 2g, Sodium 777mg

Italian-Style Pot Roast

- **2 teaspoons minced garlic**
- **1 teaspoon salt**
- **1 teaspoon dried basil**
- **1 teaspoon dried oregano**
- **¼ teaspoon red pepper flakes**
- **2½ pounds lean boneless beef bottom round rump roast**
- **1 large yellow onion, quartered and thinly sliced**
- **1½ cups marinara pasta sauce**
- **2 cans (about 15 ounces each) Great Northern beans, rinsed and drained**
- **¼ cup shredded fresh basil**

1. Combine garlic, salt, basil, oregano and pepper flakes in small bowl; rub over roast.

2. Place half of onion slices into **CROCK-POT**® slow cooker. (Cut roast in half to fit into smaller **CROCK-POT**® slow cooker.) Place one half of roast over onion slices; top with remaining onion slices and other half of roast (if using 4-quart slow cooker). Pour pasta sauce over roast. Cover; cook on LOW 8 to 9 hours or until roast is fork-tender.

3. Remove roast to cutting board; tent with foil. Let liquid in **CROCK-POT**® slow cooker stand 5 minutes to allow fat to rise. Skim off fat.

4. Stir beans into liquid. Cover; cook on HIGH 15 to 30 minutes or until beans are hot. Carve roast across the grain into thin slices. Serve with bean mixture and fresh basil.

Makes 8 servings

Nutrition Information: Serving Size about 1¼ cups, Calories 372, Total Fat 9g, Saturated Fat 3g, Protein 41g, Carbohydrate 29g, Cholesterol 84mg, Dietary Fiber 6g, Sodium 689mg

Beef Main Dishes

Peppered Brisket and Cabbage

- 12 small red new potatoes, quartered
- 4 carrots, sliced
- 1 beef brisket (about 2 pounds)
- 2 medium yellow onions, sliced
- 3 whole bay leaves
- 8 whole black peppercorns
- ½ teaspoon pickling spice
- 1 head cabbage, cut into wedges

1. Place potatoes and carrots in bottom of **CROCK-POT**® slow cooker. Add remaining ingredients except cabbage and enough water to cover brisket. Cover; cook on LOW 4 to 5 hours or on HIGH 2 to 2½ hours.

2. Add cabbage. Continue cooking on LOW 4 to 5 hours longer or on HIGH 2 to 2½ hours longer. Slice brisket against the grain, and serve with vegetables.

Makes 10 servings

Nutrition Information: Serving Size about 1½ cups, Calories 329, Total Fat 7g, Saturated Fat 2g, Protein 24g, Carbohydrate 42g, Cholesterol 56mg, Dietary Fiber 7g, Sodium 352mg

Italian Braised Short Ribs in Red Wine

3 **pounds beef short ribs, trimmed of excess fat**

Salt and black pepper

2 **large yellow onions, sliced**

2 **cloves garlic, minced**

2 **packages (8 ounces each) baby bella or cremini mushrooms, cleaned and quartered**

2 **cups red wine**

2 **cups 99% fat-free beef broth**

2 **teaspoons Italian seasoning**

Mashed potatoes or polenta

1. Coat **CROCK-POT®** slow cooker with nonstick cooking spray. Season short ribs with salt and pepper. Brown ribs on all sides in large nonstick skillet over medium-high heat, working in batches as needed. Transfer to prepared **CROCK-POT®** slow cooker as batches are finished.

2. Return skillet to heat. Add onions and cook, stirring frequently, until translucent, about 3 to 5 minutes. Stir in remaining ingredients except potatoes and bring mixture to simmer. Cook 3 minutes then pour over short ribs. Cover and cook on LOW 10 to 12 hours or on HIGH 6 to 8 hours or until beef is tender. Season to taste with salt and pepper. Transfer ribs and mushrooms to serving plate. Strain cooking liquid; serve with mashed potatoes or polenta and cooking liquid.

Makes 8 servings

Nutrition Information: Serving Size about 1 rib and ½ cup sauce, Calories 279, Total Fat 12g, Saturated Fat 4g, Protein 24g, Carbohydrate 8g, Cholesterol 67mg, Dietary Fiber 1g, Sodium 303mg

Pork Main Dishes

Sauerkraut Pork Ribs

    Nonstick cooking spray

2 **pounds country-style pork ribs**

1 **medium yellow onion, thinly sliced**

1 **teaspoon caraway seeds**

½ **teaspoon garlic powder**

¼ **teaspoon black pepper**

1 **package (about 14 ounces) fresh cole slaw mix**

¾ **cup water**

1 **can (about 14 ounces) sauerkraut**

12 **medium red potatoes, quartered**

1. Coat large nonstick skillet with cooking spray and place over medium-low heat Brown ribs on all sides. Transfer to **CROCK-POT**® slow cooker. Drain drippings from skillet and discard.

2. Add onion to skillet; cook until tender. Add caraway seeds, garlic powder and pepper; cook 15 minutes. Transfer onion mixture to **CROCK-POT**® slow cooker. Top with cole slaw mix.

3. Add water to skillet and scrape up any brown bits. Pour pan juices into **CROCK-POT**® slow cooker. Drain half of canning liquid from sauerkraut; pour sauerkraut and remaining liquid over meat. Top with potatoes. Cover; cook on LOW 6 to 8 hours or until potatoes are tender, stirring once during cooking.

Makes 6 servings

Nutrition Information: Serving Size ⅙ ribs and ¾ cup vegetable mixture, Calories 496, Total Fat 9g, Saturated Fat 2g, Protein 40g, Carbohydrate 63g, Cholesterol 112mg, Dietary Fiber 9g, Sodium 339mg

Pork Main Dishes

Pork Loin Stuffed with Stone Fruits

- 1 boneless pork loin roast (about 4 pounds)
  Salt and black pepper, to taste
- 2 tablespoons olive oil, divided
- 1 medium yellow onion, chopped
- ½ cup Madeira or sherry wine
- ½ cup dried pitted plums
- ½ cup dried peaches
- ½ cup dried apricots
- 2 cloves garlic, minced
- ¾ teaspoon salt
- ½ teaspoon black pepper
- ¼ teaspoon dried thyme

Tip

To butterfly a roast means to split the meat down the center without cutting all the way through. This allows the meat to be spread open so a filling can be added.

1. Coat **CROCK-POT®** slow cooker with nonstick cooking spray. Season pork with salt and pepper. Heat 1 tablespoon olive in large nonstick skillet over medium-high heat until hot. Sear pork on all sides, turning as it browns. Transfer to cutting board; let stand until cool enough to handle.

2. Add remaining 1 tablespoon olive oil to same skillet over medium heat. Add onion. Cook and stir until translucent. Add Madeira. Cook 2 to 3 minutes until mixture reduces slightly. Stir in dried fruit, garlic, salt, pepper and thyme. Cook 1 minute longer. Remove skillet from heat.

3. Butterfly roast lengthwise (use sharp knife to cut meat; cut to within 1½ inches of edge). Spread roast flat on cutting board, browned side down. Spoon fruit mixture onto pork roast. Bring sides together to close roast. Slide kitchen string under roast and tie roast shut, allowing 2 inches between ties. If any fruit escapes, push back gently. Place roast in **CROCK-POT®** slow cooker. Cover; cook on LOW 5 to 6 hours or on HIGH 2 to 3 hours, or until roast is tender.

4. Transfer roast to cutting board and let stand 10 minutes. Pour cooking liquid into small saucepan (strain through fine-mesh sieve first, if desired). Cook over high heat about 3 minutes to reduce sauce. Add salt and pepper to sauce, if desired. Slice roast and serve with sauce.

Makes 10 servings

Nutrition Information: Serving Size ⅒ roast and about ¾ cup fruit and sauce, Calories 319, Total Fat 11g, Saturated Fat 3g, Protein 39g, Carbohydrate 14g, Cholesterol 114mg, Dietary Fiber 2g, Sodium 270mg

Pecan and Apple Stuffed Pork Chops with Apple Brandy

4 **thick-cut, bone-in pork loin chops (about 12 ounces each)**

1 **teaspoon salt, divided**

½ **teaspoon black pepper, divided**

2 **tablespoons vegetable oil**

½ **cup diced green apple**

½ **small yellow onion, minced**

¼ **teaspoon dried thyme**

½ **cup apple brandy or brandy**

⅔ **cup cubed white bread**

1 **tablespoon chopped pecans**

1 **cup apple juice**

1. Coat **CROCK-POT®** slow cooker with nonstick cooking spray; set aside. Rinse pork chops and pat dry. Season with ½ teaspoon salt and ¼ teaspoon pepper. Heat oil in large skillet over medium-high heat until hot. Sear pork chops about 2 minutes on both sides or until browned. Cook in 2 batches, if necessary; set aside.

2. Add apple, onion, thyme, remaining ½ teaspoon salt and remaining ¼ teaspoon pepper to hot skillet and reduce heat to medium. Cook and stir 3 minutes or until onion is translucent. Remove from heat and pour in brandy. Return to medium heat and simmer until most of liquid is absorbed. Stir in bread and pecans, and cook 1 minute longer.

3. Cut each pork chop horizontally with sharp knife to form pocket. Divide stuffing among pork chops. Arrange pork chops in **CROCK-POT®** slow cooker, pocket side up.

4. Pour apple juice around pork chops. Cover; cook on HIGH 1½ to 1¾ hours or until pork is 155°F when measured with meat thermometer.

Makes 4 servings

Nutrition Information: Serving Size 1 pork chop and about ⅓ cup stuffing, Calories 415, Total Fat 11g, Saturated Fat 3g, Protein 42g, Carbohydrate 13g, Cholesterol 122mg, Dietary Fiber 1g, Sodium 720mg

# Pork Main Dishes

Rigatoni with Broccoli Rabe and Sausage

    2   tablespoons olive oil, plus more for oiling stoneware insert
    3   sweet or hot Italian sausage links, casings removed
    2   cloves garlic, minced
    1   large bunch (about 1¼ pounds) broccoli rabe
    ½   cup 99% fat-free chicken broth or water
    ½   teaspoon salt
    ½   teaspoon red pepper flakes
    1   pound uncooked rigatoni
        Grated Parmesan cheese (optional)

1. Lightly coat interior of **CROCK-POT®** slow cooker with nonstick cooking spray. Set aside.

2. Heat 2 tablespoons oil in large skillet over medium heat. Add sausage and cook, stirring to break up sausage with spoon, until lightly browned, about 6 minutes. Add garlic and stir until softened and fragrant, about 1 minute. Transfer to lightly prepared **CROCK-POT®** slow cooker.

3. Trim any stiff, woody parts from bottoms of broccoli rabe stems and discard. Cut broccoli rabe into 1-inch lengths. Place in large bowl of cold water. Stir with hands to wash well. Lift broccoli rabe out of water by handfuls leaving any sand or dirt in bottom of bowl. Shake well to remove excess water, but do not dry. Add to **CROCK-POT®** slow cooker with sausage. Pour in broth and sprinkle with salt and red pepper flakes. Cover; cook on LOW 4 hours or on HIGH 2 hours.

4. Meanwhile, cook rigatoni according to package directions. Stir into sausage mixture just before serving. Serve garnished, as desired, with Parmesan cheese.

Makes 6 servings

Nutrition Information: Serving Size about 1½ cups, Calories 414, Total Fat 10g, Saturated Fat 3g, Protein 21g, Carbohydrate 62g, Cholesterol 13mg, Dietary Fiber 2g, Sodium 545mg

Golden Harvest Pork Stew

 1 **pound boneless pork loin rib roast, cut into 1-inch pieces**

 2 **tablespoons all-purpose flour, divided**

 1 **tablespoon vegetable oil**

 2 **medium Yukon Gold potatoes, unpeeled and cut into 1-inch cubes**

 1 **large sweet potato, peeled and cut into 1-inch cubes**

 1 **cup chopped carrots**

 1 **ear corn, broken into 4 pieces or ½ cup corn kernels**

 ½ **cup 99% fat-free, reduced-sodium chicken broth**

 1 **jalapeño pepper, seeded and finely chopped***

 1 **clove garlic, minced**

 1 **teaspoon salt**

 ¼ **teaspoon black pepper**

 ¼ **teaspoon dried thyme**

    Chopped parsley

*Jalapeño peppers can sting and irritate the skin, so wear rubber gloves when handling peppers and do not touch your eyes.

1. Toss pork pieces with 1 tablespoon flour; set aside. Heat oil in large skillet over medium-high heat until hot. Add pork; cook until browned on all sides. Transfer to **CROCK-POT®** slow cooker.

2. Add remaining ingredients, except parsley, and 1 tablespoon flour. Cover; cook on LOW 5 to 6 hours.

3. Combine remaining 1 tablespoon flour and ¼ cup cooking liquid from stew in small bowl; stir until smooth. Stir flour mixture into stew. Cook on HIGH 10 minutes or until thickened. To serve, sprinkle with parsley.

Makes 4 servings

Nutrition Information: Serving Size about 1½ cups, Calories 329, Total Fat 7g, Saturated Fat 2g, Protein 30g, Carbohydrate 35g, Cholesterol 65mg, Dietary Fiber 5g, Sodium 751mg

Pork Main Dishes

Boneless Pork Roast with Garlic

1 **lean boneless pork rib roast (2 to 2½ pounds), rinsed and patted dry**

   Salt and black pepper, to taste

3 **tablespoons olive oil, divided**

4 **cloves garlic, minced**

4 **tablespoons chopped fresh rosemary**

½ **lemon, cut into ⅛- to ¼-inch slices**

¼ **cup white wine (such as Chardonnay)**

½ **cup 99% fat-free chicken stock**

1. Unroll the pork roast and season with salt and pepper. Combine 2 tablespoons oil, garlic and rosemary in small bowl. Rub over pork.

2. Roll and tie pork snugly with twine. Tuck lemon slices under twine and into ends of roast.

3. Heat remaining 1 tablespoon oil in skillet over medium heat until hot. Sear pork on all sides until just browned. Transfer to **CROCK-POT®** slow cooker.

4. Return skillet to heat. Add white wine and stock, stirring with wooden spoon to loosen any caramelized bits. Pour over pork. Cover; cook on LOW 8 to 9 hours or on HIGH 3½ to 4 hours.

5. Transfer roast to cutting board. Allow to rest for 10 minutes before removing twine and slicing. Adjust seasonings, if desired. To serve, pour pan juices over sliced pork.

Makes 6 servings

Nutrition Information: Serving Size ⅙ roast, Calories 273, Total Fat 12g, Saturated Fat 3g, Protein 35g, Carbohydrate 2g, Cholesterol 86mg, Dietary Fiber 0g, Sodium 162mg

Pork Main Dishes

Posole

 3 **pounds boneless pork, cubed**

 2 **cans (14 ounces each) white hominy, drained**

 1 **package (10 ounces) frozen white corn kernels, thawed**

 ¾ **cup chili sauce**

Combine all ingredients in **CROCK-POT®** slow cooker. Cover; cook on HIGH 5 hours. Reduce temperature to LOW. Cook on LOW 10 hours.

Makes 8 servings

Nutrition Information: Serving Size about 1½ cups, Calories 344, Total Fat 6g, Saturated Fat 2g, Protein 42g, Carbohydrate 27g, Cholesterol 97mg, Dietary Fiber 5g, Sodium 646mg

German Kraut and Sausage

 5 **medium potatoes, cut into ½-inch pieces**

 1 **large yellow onion, cut into ¼-inch slices**

 ½ **green bell pepper, chopped**

 1 **can (16 ounces) sauerkraut**

 1 **pound reduced-fat smoked sausage, cut into 1-inch pieces**

 ¼ **cup packed brown sugar**

 1 **teaspoon garlic powder**

 ½ **teaspoon black pepper**

1. Place potatoes in **CROCK-POT®** slow cooker. Layer onion, bell pepper and sauerkraut over top.

2. Brown sausage in large skillet over medium-high heat. Transfer to **CROCK-POT®** slow cooker.

3. Combine brown sugar, garlic powder and black pepper in small bowl. Sprinkle over sausage.

4. Cover; cook on LOW 8 hours or until potatoes are tender.

Makes 8 servings

Nutrition Information: Serving Size about 1½ cups, Calories 282, Total Fat 11g, Saturated Fat 4g, Protein 13g, Carbohydrate 34g, Cholesterol 41mg, Dietary Fiber 5g, Sodium 550mg

Posole

Pork Main Dishes

Pork Roast with Fruit Medley

- 1 **lean bone-in center-cut loin pork roast (about 4 pounds)**
- ¾ **tablespoon salt**
- 1 **tablespoon black pepper**
- 2 **cups green grapes**
- 1 **cup dried apricots**
- 1 **cup dried prunes**
- 2 **whole bay leaves**
- 1 **teaspoon dried thyme**
- 2 **cloves garlic, minced**
- 1 **cup red wine**
-    **Juice of ½ lemon**

1. Season pork roast all over with salt and pepper. Coat large nonstick skillet with nonstick cooking spray and place over medium-high heat. Place roast in pan and cook until brown, about 5 minutes. Turn to brown all sides. Remove from heat; set aside.

2. Combine remaining ingredients in **CROCK-POT®** slow cooker. Stir gently to combine.

3. Add pork roast to **CROCK-POT®** slow cooker. Turn to coat with sauce. Cover; cook on LOW 7 to 9 hours or on HIGH 3 to 5 hours.

Makes 8 servings

Nutrition Information: Serving Size ⅛ roast and ¾ cup fruit sauce, Calories 441, Total Fat 10g, Saturated Fat 3g, Protein 49g, Carbohydrate 32g, Cholesterol 142mg, Dietary Fiber 3g, Sodium 776mg

Pork Main Dishes

Simply Delicious Pork Roast

- 1½ **pounds boneless pork loin, cut into 6 pieces or 6 boneless pork loin chops**
- 4 **medium Golden Delicious apples, cored and sliced**
- 3 **tablespoons packed light brown sugar**
- 1 **teaspoon ground cinnamon**
- ½ **teaspoon salt**

1. Place pork in **CROCK-POT®** slow cooker. Cover with apples.

2. Combine brown sugar, cinnamon and salt in small bowl; sprinkle over apples. Cover; cook on LOW 6 to 8 hours.

Makes 6 servings

Nutrition Information: Serving Size ⅙ pork and about 1 cup sauce, Calories 222, Total Fat 4g, Saturated Fat 1g, Protein 26g, Carbohydrate 21g, Cholesterol 65mg, Dietary Fiber 2g, Sodium 259mg

Ham and Potato Casserole

- 1½ **pounds red potatoes, peeled and sliced**
- 8 **ounces thinly sliced extra-lean deli ham**
- 2 **poblano chile peppers, cut into thin strips**
- 2 **tablespoons olive oil**
- 1 **tablespoon dried oregano leaves**
- ¼ **teaspoon salt**
- 1 **cup (4 ounces) shredded Monterey Jack cheese**
- 2 **tablespoons finely chopped fresh cilantro**

1. Combine all ingredients except cheese and cilantro in **CROCK-POT®** slow cooker; mix well. Cover; cook on LOW 7 hours or on HIGH 4 hours.

2. Transfer potato mixture to serving dish; sprinkle with cheese and cilantro. Let stand 3 minutes or until cheese melts.

Makes 6 to 7 servings

Nutrition Information: Serving Size ½ casserole, Calories 201, Total Fat 10g, Saturated Fat 4g, Protein 12g, Carbohydrate 17g, Cholesterol 32mg, Dietary Fiber 2g, Sodium 543mg

**Simply Delicious
Pork Roast**

Pork Main Dishes

Braised Pork Shanks with Israeli Couscous and Root Vegetable Stew

 4 pork shanks, bone in, skin removed (about 1½ pounds total)
   Coarse salt and black pepper, to taste
 2 tablespoons olive oil
 4 large carrots, peeled and sliced diagonally into 1-inch pieces, divided
 4 stalks celery, sliced diagonally into 1-inch pieces, divided
 1 large yellow onion, peeled and quartered
 4 cloves garlic, peeled and crushed
 4 cups fat-free, reduced-sodium chicken broth
 2 cups dry white wine
 ¼ cup no-salt-added tomato paste
 ¼ cup distilled white vinegar
 2 tablespoons mustard oil* (optional)
 1 tablespoon whole black peppercorns
   Israeli Couscous (recipe follows)

Mustard oil is available at Middle Eastern specialty shops or in the supermarket ethnic foods aisle.

1. Season shanks well with salt and pepper. Heat oil in large skillet over medium heat until hot. Brown shanks on all sides, turning as they brown. Transfer to **CROCK-POT®** slow cooker.

2. Pour off all but 2 tablespoons oil in skillet. Add half of carrots, half of celery, onion and garlic. Cook and stir over medium-low heat until vegetables are soft but not brown, about 5 minutes. Transfer to **CROCK-POT®** slow cooker.

3. Add broth, wine, tomato paste, vinegar, mustard oil, if desired, and peppercorns to skillet. Bring to a boil, stirring and scraping up any browned bits in bottom of pan. Pour over shanks. Cover; cook on HIGH 2 hours, turning shanks every 20 minutes or so.

4. Remove shanks. Strain cooking liquid and discard solids. Return cooking liquid to **CROCK-POT®** slow cooker. Add remaining carrots and celery, and return shanks to **CROCK-POT®** slow cooker. Cover; cook on HIGH 1 hour.

5. Check shanks for doneness: remove one and place it on a plate. Meat should be very soft but still attached to bone.

6. To serve; add cooked couscous to **CROCK-POT®** slow cooker to reheat on HIGH 3 to 4 minutes. Using a slotted spoon, place couscous, carrots and celery in shallow bowls. Place shank on top and spoon 2 to 3 ounces of cooking liquid into bowl.

Makes 4 servings

Nutrition Information: Serving Size 1 pork shank and 1 cup stew, Calories 459, Total Fat 12g, Saturated Fat 3g, Protein 31g, Carbohydrate 44g, Cholesterol 68mg, Dietary Fiber 5g, Sodium 488mg

Israeli Couscous

> **2 cups water**
>
> **Pinch salt**
>
> **1⅓ cups Israeli or regular couscous**

1. Place water and salt in skillet over medium-low heat. Bring to a boil.

2. Add Israeli couscous and cook, stirring until tender, about 6 to 8 minutes. (If using regular couscous, prepare using package directions.) Drain and use immediately or rinse under cold water and reserve for later use.

Italian-Style Sausage with Rice

1 pound mild Italian sausage links, cut into 1-inch pieces

1 can (about 15 ounces) no-salt-added pinto beans, rinsed and drained

1 cup reduced-sodium marinara sauce

1 green bell pepper, cut into strips

1 small yellow onion, halved and sliced

½ teaspoon salt

¼ teaspoon black pepper

   Hot cooked rice

   Fresh basil (optional)

1. Cook sausage in large nonstick skillet over medium-high heat, stirring to break up meat, until cooked through. Drain fat.

2. Place sausage, beans, pasta sauce, bell pepper, onion, salt and black pepper in **CROCK-POT®** slow cooker. Cover; cook on LOW 4 to 6 hours or on HIGH 2 to 3 hours.

3. Serve with rice. Garnish with basil, if desired.

Makes 5 servings

Nutrition Information: Serving Size about 1½ cups, Calories 267, Total Fat 8g, Saturated Fat 3g, Protein 19g, Carbohydrate 19g, Cholesterol 27mg, Dietary Fiber 5g, Sodium 800mg

Pork Roast Landaise

>   2 **tablespoons olive oil**
>   2½ **pounds boneless center-cut pork loin roast**
>   **Salt and black pepper, to taste**
>   1 **medium yellow onion, diced**
>   2 **large cloves garlic, minced**
>   2 **teaspoons dried thyme**
>   2 **parsnips, cut into ¾-inch slices**
>   ¼ **cup red wine vinegar**
>   ¼ **cup sugar**
>   ½ **cup sherry wine**
>   2 **cups 99% fat-free chicken broth, divided**
>   2 **tablespoons cornstarch**
>   3 **pears, cored and sliced ¾ inch thick**
>   1½ **cups pitted prunes**

1. Heat oil in large saucepan over medium-high heat. Season pork roast with salt and pepper; brown roast on all sides in saucepan. Place roast in **CROCK-POT®** slow cooker.

2. Add onion and garlic to saucepan. Cook and stir over medium heat 2 to 3 minutes. Stir in thyme. Transfer to **CROCK-POT®** slow cooker. Add parsnips; stir well.

3. Combine vinegar and sugar in same saucepan. Cook over medium heat, stirring constantly, until mixture thickens into syrup. Add sherry and cook 1 minute more. Add 1¾ cups chicken broth. Combine remaining ¼ cup of broth with cornstarch in small bowl. Whisk in cornstarch mixture, and cook until smooth and slightly thickened. Pour into **CROCK-POT®** slow cooker.

4. Cover; cook on LOW 8 hours or on HIGH 4 hours. Add pears and prunes during last 30 minutes of cooking.

Makes 8 servings

Nutrition Information: Serving Size ⅛ roast and about ½ cup sauce, Calories 407, Total Fat 9g, Saturated Fat 2g, Protein 33g, Carbohydrate 45g, Cholesterol 98mg, Dietary Fiber 5g, Sodium 325mg

Pork Main Dishes

Pork Loin with Sherry and Red Onions

 3 **large red onions, thinly sliced**

 1 **cup pearl onions, blanched and peeled**

 1 **tablespoon unsalted butter**

2½ **pounds boneless pork loin, tied**

 ½ **teaspoon salt**

 ½ **teaspoon freshly ground black pepper**

 ½ **cup cooking sherry**

 2 **tablespoons fresh chopped Italian parsley**

1½ **tablespoons cornstarch**

 2 **tablespoons water**

Note

The mild flavor of pork is awakened by this rich, delectable sauce.

1. Cook red and pearl onions in butter in medium skillet over medium heat until soft.

2. Rub pork loin with salt and pepper and place in **CROCK-POT®** slow cooker. Add cooked onions, sherry and parsley. Cover; cook on LOW 8 to 10 hours or on HIGH 5 to 6 hours.

3. Remove pork loin; cover and let stand 15 minutes before slicing.

4. Turn heat to HIGH. Combine cornstarch and water and stir into cooking liquid in **CROCK-POT®** slow cooker. Cook 15 minutes or until sauce has thickened. Serve sliced pork loin with onions and sherry sauce.

Makes 8 servings

Nutrition Information: Serving Size ⅛ roast and about ¼ cup sauce, Calories 253, Total Fat 6g, Saturated Fat 3g, Protein 34g, Carbohydrate 13g, Cholesterol 84mg, Dietary Fiber 1g, Sodium 412mg

Mediterranean Meatball Ratatouille

- 1 **pound reduced-fat mild Italian sausage**
- 1 **package (8 ounces) sliced mushrooms**
- 1 **small eggplant, diced**
- 1 **zucchini, diced**
- ½ **cup chopped yellow onion**
- 1 **clove garlic, minced**
- 1 **teaspoon dried oregano**
- 1 **teaspoon salt**
- ½ **teaspoon black pepper**
- 2 **tomatoes, diced**
- 1 **tablespoon tomato paste**
- 2 **tablespoons chopped fresh basil**
- 1 **teaspoon fresh lemon juice**

1. Shape sausage into 1-inch meatballs. Brown meatballs in large skillet over medium heat. Place half the meatballs in **CROCK-POT**® slow cooker. Add half each of mushrooms, eggplant and zucchini. Top with onion, garlic, ½ teaspoon oregano, ½ teaspoon salt and ¼ teaspoon pepper.

2. Add remaining meatballs, mushrooms, eggplant and zucchini, ½ teaspoon oregano, ½ teaspoon salt and ¼ teaspoon pepper. Cover; cook on LOW 6 to 7 hours.

3. Stir in diced tomatoes and tomato paste. Cover; cook on LOW 15 minutes. Stir in basil and lemon juice just before serving.

Makes 6 (1⅔-cup) servings

Nutrition Information: Serving Size 1⅔ cups, Calories 173, Total Fat 11g, Saturated Fat 4g, Protein 12g, Carbohydrate 9g, Cholesterol 41mg, Dietary Fiber 3g, Sodium 676mg

Pork Main Dishes

Panama Pork Stew

- 2 small sweet potatoes (about ¾ pound), peeled and cut into 2-inch pieces
- 1 package (10 ounces) frozen corn
- 1 package (9 ounces) frozen cut green beans
- 1 cup chopped yellow onion
- 1¼ pounds pork top loin roast, cut into 1-inch cubes
- 1 can (14½ ounces) diced tomatoes, undrained
- ¼ cup water
- 1 tablespoon chili powder
- ½ teaspoon salt
- ½ teaspoon ground coriander

1. Place potatoes, corn, green beans and onion in **CROCK-POT®** slow cooker. Top with pork.

2. Combine tomatoes with juice, water, chili powder, salt and coriander in medium bowl. Pour over pork. Cover; cook on LOW 7 to 9 hours.

Makes 6 servings

Nutrition Information: Serving Size about 1¼ cups, Calories 243, Total Fat 4g, Saturated Fat 1g, Protein 25g, Carbohydrate 26g, Cholesterol 60mg, Dietary Fiber 5g, Sodium 494mg

Pork Chops with Dried Fruit and Onions

**6 bone-in end-cut pork chops
(about 2½ pounds)**

Salt and black pepper, to taste

3 tablespoons vegetable oil

2 medium yellow onions, diced

2 cloves garlic, minced

¼ teaspoon dried sage

¾ cup quartered pitted dried plums

¾ cup chopped mixed dried fruit

**3 cups unsweetened unfiltered
apple juice**

1 bay leaf

1. Season pork chops with salt and pepper. Heat oil in large skillet over medium-high heat until hot. Sear pork on both sides to brown, cooking in batches, if necessary. Transfer to **CROCK-POT®** slow cooker.

2. Add onions to hot skillet. Cook and stir over medium heat until softened. Add garlic and cook 30 seconds more. Sprinkle sage over mixture. Add dried plums, mixed fruit and apple juice. Bring mixture to a boil. Reduce heat and simmer, uncovered, 3 minutes, scraping bottom and sides of pan to release browned bits. Ladle mixture over pork chops.

3. Add bay leaf. Cover; cook on LOW 3½ to 4 hours, or until pork chops are tender. Remove bay leaf. Add salt and pepper, if desired. To serve, spoon fruit and cooking liquid over pork chops.

Makes 6 servings

Nutrition Information: Serving Size 1 pork chop and ½ cup fruit and onions, Calories 359, Total Fat 11g, Saturated Fat 3g, Protein 24g, Carbohydrate 41g, Cholesterol 63mg, Dietary Fiber 3g, Sodium 91mg

Pork Main Dishes

Pork and Tomato Ragoût

   2 **pounds lean pork top loin roast, cut into 1-inch pieces**

  ¼ **cup all-purpose flour**

   2 **tablespoons olive oil**

1¼ **cups white wine**

   2 **pounds red potatoes, cut into ½-inch pieces**

   1 **can (14½ ounces) diced tomatoes, undrained**

   1 **cup finely chopped yellow onion**

   1 **cup water**

  ½ **cup finely chopped celery**

   2 **cloves garlic, minced**

  ½ **teaspoon black pepper**

   1 **cinnamon stick**

   3 **tablespoons chopped fresh parsley**

Tip

Vegetables such as potatoes and carrots can sometimes take longer to cook in a CROCK-POT® slow cooker than meat. Place evenly cut vegetables along the sides of the CROCK-POT® slow cooker when possible.

1. Toss pork with flour. Heat oil in large skillet over medium-high heat until hot. Add pork to skillet and brown on all sides. Transfer to **CROCK-POT®** slow cooker.

2. Add wine to skillet; bring to a boil, scraping up browned bits from bottom of skillet. Pour into **CROCK-POT®** slow cooker.

3. Add all remaining ingredients except parsley. Cover; cook on LOW 6 to 8 hours or until pork and potatoes are tender. Remove and discard cinnamon stick. Adjust seasonings, if desired. To serve, sprinkle with parsley.

Makes 8 servings

Nutrition Information: Serving Size about 1¼ cups, Calories 323, Total Fat 8g, Saturated Fat 2g, Protein 29g, Carbohydrate 27g, Cholesterol 71mg, Dietary Fiber 3g, Sodium 212mg

Pork Chops à l'Orange

- 1 **tablespoon extra-virgin olive oil**
- 8 **lean boneless center-cut pork loin chops**
- ⅓ **cup orange juice**
- 2 **tablespoons clover honey**
- 1 **teaspoon salt**
- 1 **teaspoon packed brown sugar**
- 1 **teaspoon grated orange peel**
- 2 **tablespoons cornstarch**
- ¼ **cup water**

1. Heat oil in large skillet over medium-high heat until hot. Working in batches, sear chops on both sides about 1 to 2 minutes, turning each chop as it browns; set aside.

2. Combine orange juice, honey, salt, brown sugar and orange peel in **CROCK-POT**® slow cooker. Add chops, turning each chop to coat well. Cover; cook on LOW 6 to 8 hours.

3. Transfer chops to warm plate. Pour cooking liquid into small heavy saucepan. Cook over medium-high heat until liquid begins to boil. Meanwhile, combine cornstarch and water in small bowl. Add to orange sauce. Stir well to combine. Reduce heat and simmer 5 minutes, or until thickened. Spoon sauce over chops, and serve immediately.

Makes 8 servings

Nutrition Information: Serving Size 1 pork chop and 1½ tablespoons sauce, Calories 197, Total Fat 7g, Saturated Fat 2g, Protein 23g, Carbohydrate 7g, Cholesterol 63mg, Dietary Fiber 0g, Sodium 347mg

Pork Main Dishes

Lemon Pork Chops

1   **tablespoon vegetable oil**

4   **lean boneless pork loin chops**

3   **cans (8 ounces each) no-salt-added tomato sauce**

1   **large yellow onion, quartered and sliced (optional)**

1   **large green bell pepper, cut into strips**

1   **tablespoon lemon-pepper seasoning**

1   **tablespoon Worcestershire sauce**

1   **large lemon, quartered**

   Lemon wedges (optional)

Tip

Browning pork before adding it to the **CROCK-POT®** slow cooker helps reduce the fat. Just remember to drain off the fat in the skillet before transferring the pork to the **CROCK-POT®** slow cooker.

1. Heat oil in large skillet over medium-low heat until hot. Brown pork chops on both sides. Drain excess fat and discard. Transfer to **CROCK-POT®** slow cooker.

2. Combine tomato sauce, onion, if desired, bell pepper, lemon-pepper seasoning and Worcestershire sauce. Add to **CROCK-POT®** slow cooker.

3. Squeeze juice from lemon quarters over mixture; drop squeezed lemons into **CROCK-POT®** slow cooker. Cover; cook on LOW 6 to 8 hours or until pork is tender. Remove squeezed lemons before serving. Garnish with additional lemon wedges, if desired.

Makes 4 servings

Nutrition Information: Serving Size 1 pork chop and about ½ cup sauce, Calories 279, Total Fat 10g, Saturated Fat 2g, Protein 26g, Carbohydrate 21g, Cholesterol 63mg, Dietary Fiber 4g, Sodium 332mg

Ham with Fruited Bourbon Sauce

- 1 **fully cooked bone-in ham (about 6 pounds)**
- ¾ **cup packed dark brown sugar**
- ½ **cup raisins**
- ½ **cup apple juice**
- 1 **teaspoon ground cinnamon**
- ¼ **teaspoon red pepper flakes**
- ⅓ **cup dried cherries**
- ¼ **cup bourbon, rum or apple juice**
- ¼ **cup cornstarch**

1. Coat **CROCK-POT**® slow cooker with nonstick cooking spray. Add ham, cut side up. Combine brown sugar, raisins, apple juice, cinnamon and red pepper flakes in small bowl; stir well. Pour over ham. Cover; cook on LOW 9 to 10 hours or on HIGH 4½ to 5 hours. Add cherries 30 minutes before end of cooking time.

2. Transfer ham to cutting board. Cover and let stand 15 minutes before slicing.

3. Meanwhile, pour cooking liquid into large measuring cup. Let stand 5 minutes; skim and discard fat. Return cooking liquid to **CROCK-POT**® slow cooker.

4. Turn **CROCK-POT**® slow cooker to HIGH. Stir bourbon into cornstarch in small bowl until smooth. Stir into cooking liquid. Cover; cook 15 minutes or until thickened. Serve sauce over ham.

Makes 12 servings

Nutrition Information: Serving Size ½₂ ham and about ¼ cup sauce, Calories 423, Total Fat 12g, Saturated Fat 4g, Protein 47g, Carbohydrate 26g, Cholesterol 154mg, Dietary Fiber 1g, Sodium 131mg

Pork Main Dishes

Andouille and Cabbage Crock

- 1 **pound andouille sausage, cut into 3- to 4-inch pieces**
- 1 **small head cabbage, cut in 8 wedges (about 1 pound total)**
- 1 **medium onion, cut in ½-inch wedges**
- 3 **medium carrots, peeled, quartered lengthwise, and cut into 3-inch pieces**
- 8 **new potatoes, cut in half (about 1 pound total)**
- ½ **cup apple juice**
- 1 **can (14 ounces) 99% fat-free, reduced-sodium chicken broth**

   Honey mustard and crusty rolls (optional)

Tip

Andouille is a spicy, smoked pork sausage. Feel free to substitute your favorite smoked sausage or kielbasa.

1. Cook sausage in large skillet coated with nonstick cooking spray over medium-high heat. Stir sausage frequently until brown on both sides. Remove from heat; set aside.

2. Coat **CROCK-POT**® slow cooker with cooking spray. Place all ingredients except honey mustard and rolls in **CROCK-POT**® slow cooker, with sausage on top. Cover. Cook on HIGH for 3½ hours. Stir gently, making sure vegetables are covered with liquid. Cook 30 minutes more or until cabbage is tender. Remove with slotted spoon. Serve with honey mustard and crusty rolls, if desired.

Makes about 8 servings

Nutrition Information: Serving Size 1½ cups, Calories 290, Total Fat 11g, Saturated Fat 4g, Protein 14g, Carbohydrate 38g, Cholesterol 32mg, Dietary Fiber 7g, Sodium 588mg

Cajun-Style Country Ribs

    2   **cups baby carrots**

    1   **medium onion, coarsely chopped**

    1   **green bell pepper, cut into 1-inch pieces**

    1   **red bell pepper, cut into 1-inch pieces**

    2   **teaspoons minced garlic**

    2   **tablespoons Creole seasoning, divided**

    3   **pounds lean pork country-style spareribs**

    1   **can (about 14 ounces) no-salt-added stewed tomatoes, undrained**

    2   **tablespoons water**

    1   **tablespoon cornstarch**

        Hot cooked rice

1. Combine carrots, onion, bell peppers, garlic and 2 teaspoons seasoning in **CROCK-POT**® slow cooker; mix well.

2. Trim excess fat from ribs; cut into individual ribs. Sprinkle with 1 tablespoon seasoning; place in **CROCK-POT**® slow cooker. Pour tomatoes over ribs. Cover; cook on LOW 6 to 8 hours.

3. Remove ribs and vegetables from **CROCK-POT**® slow cooker with slotted spoon. Let liquid stand 15 minutes; skim off fat.

4. Turn to HIGH. Stir water into cornstarch and remaining 1 teaspoon seasoning in small bowl until smooth. Stir into **CROCK-POT**® slow cooker. Cook, uncovered, 15 minutes or until thickened. Return ribs and vegetables to sauce; carefully stir to coat. Serve with rice.

Makes 8 servings

Nutrition Information: Serving Size ⅛ ribs and about ½ cup vegetables, Calories 286, Total Fat 10g, Saturated Fat 2g, Protein 36g, Carbohydrate 10g, Cholesterol 126mg, Dietary Fiber 2g, Sodium 587mg

Poultry Main Dishes

East Indian Curried Chicken with Capers and Brown Rice

  2 **cups ripe plum tomatoes, diced**
  1 **cup artichoke hearts, drained and chopped**
  1 **cup 99% fat-free chicken broth**
  1 **medium red onion, chopped**
  ⅓ **cup dry white wine**
  ¼ **cup capers, drained**
  2 **tablespoons quick-cooking tapioca**
  2 **teaspoons curry powder**
  ½ **teaspoon ground thyme**
  ¼ **teaspoon salt**
  ¼ **teaspoon black pepper**
1½ **pounds boneless, skinless chicken breasts**
  4 **cups cooked brown rice**

1. Combine tomatoes, artichokes, broth, onion, wine and capers in **CROCK-POT®** slow cooker.

2. Combine tapioca, curry powder, thyme, salt and pepper in small bowl. Add to **CROCK-POT®** slow cooker. Stir well to combine. Add chicken. Spoon sauce over chicken to coat. Cover; cook on LOW 7 to 9 hours or on HIGH 3 to 4 hours.

3. Serve chicken and vegetables over rice. Spoon sauce over chicken.

Makes 6 servings

Nutrition Information: Serving Size about 1½ cups, Calories 327, Total Fat 4g, Saturated Fat 1g, Protein 30g, Carbohydrate 41g, Cholesterol 73mg, Dietary Fiber 4g, Sodium 648mg

Cuban-Style Curried Turkey

  2 **tablespoons all-purpose flour**

  ½ **teaspoon salt, or to taste**

  ¼ **teaspoon black pepper**

  1 **pound boneless turkey breast meat,* cut into 1-inch cubes**

  2 **tablespoons vegetable oil, divided**

  1 **small yellow onion, chopped**

  1 **clove garlic, minced**

  1 **can (15 ounces) 50% less sodium black beans, rinsed and drained**

  1 **can (about 14 ounces) no-salt-added diced tomatoes**

  ½ **cup 99% fat-free, reduced-sodium chicken broth**

  ⅓ **cup raisins**

  ¼ **teaspoon curry powder**

  ⅛ **teaspoon red pepper flakes**

     Juice of ½ lime (1 tablespoon)

  1 **tablespoon minced fresh cilantro (optional)**

  1 **tablespoon minced green onion (optional)**

  2 **cups cooked rice (optional)**

*You may substitute turkey tenderloins; cut as directed.

1. Combine flour, salt and black pepper in resealable food storage bag. Add turkey; shake well to coat. Heat 1 tablespoon oil in large skillet over medium heat. Add turkey. Cook, turning to brown all sides. Transfer to **CROCK-POT®** slow cooker.

2. Heat remaining 1 tablespoon oil in skillet. Add onion; cook and stir over medium heat 3 minutes or until golden. Stir in garlic; cook an additional 30 seconds. Transfer to **CROCK-POT®** slow cooker.

3. Stir in beans, tomatoes, broth, raisins, curry powder and red pepper flakes. Cover; cook on LOW 4 to 6 hours. Adjust seasonings; stir in lime juice. Garnish with cilantro and green onion, if desired. Serve over rice, if desired.

Makes 4 servings

Nutrition Information: Serving Size about 1¾ cups, Calories 328, Total Fat 8g, Saturated Fat 1g, Protein 32g, Carbohydrate 34g, Cholesterol 56mg, Dietary Fiber 6g, Sodium 690mg

Chicken Gumbo over Rice

  2 **tablespoons olive oil**

 ½ **pound Italian sausage, cut into ¼-inch slices**

 ¼ **cup all-purpose flour**

  1 **pound boneless, skinless chicken breasts, cut into ½-inch slices**

  1 **cup chopped yellow onion**

  1 **cup chopped celery**

  1 **cup diced green bell pepper**

  2 **tablespoons minced jalapeño or serrano peppers***

  1 **teaspoon paprika**

1½ **cups frozen okra**

  1 **cup 99% fat-free chicken broth**

 ½ **cup white wine**

  2 **cups cooked white or brown rice**

Jalapeño and serrano peppers can sting and irritate the skin, so wear rubber gloves when handling peppers and do not touch your eyes.

1. Spray large nonstick skillet with cooking spray and place over medium heat. Add sausage and cook, turning to brown both sides, about 10 minutes. Transfer to paper towel-lined plate with slotted spoon to drain.

2. Heat olive oil in same skillet. Add flour and continuously stir with a whisk. Cook until flour becomes dark brown but not burnt. Add chicken, onion, celery, bell pepper, jalapeño peppers and paprika. Cook and stir 7 to 8 minutes, or until vegetables soften. Transfer to **CROCK-POT®** slow cooker.

3. Add drained sausage, okra, broth and wine. Cover; cook on LOW 7 to 8 hours or on HIGH 4 to 6 hours. Serve over cooked rice.

Makes 6 servings

Nutrition Information: Serving Size about 1¼ cups, Calories 441, Total Fat 24g, Saturated Fat 7g, Protein 25g, Carbohydrate 26g, Cholesterol 77mg, Dietary Fiber 2g, Sodium 608mg

Creole Vegetables and Chicken

1 can (14½ ounces) no-salt-added diced tomatoes, undrained

8 ounces frozen cut okra

2 cups chopped green bell peppers

1 cup chopped yellow onion

¾ cup sliced celery

1 cup fat-free, low-sodium chicken broth

2 teaspoons Worcestershire sauce

1 teaspoon dried thyme

1 bay leaf

1 pound chicken tenders, cut into bite-size pieces

¾ teaspoon Creole seasoning

1½ teaspoons sugar

1 tablespoon extra-virgin olive oil

Hot pepper sauce, to taste

¼ cup chopped parsley

Tip

To slightly thicken stews in the **CROCK-POT®** slow cooker, remove the solid foods and leave the cooking liquid in the stoneware. Mix 2 to 4 tablespoons cornstarch with ¼ cup cold water until smooth. Stir this mixture into the **CROCK-POT®** slow cooker and cook on **HIGH** until the mixture is smooth.

1. Coat **CROCK-POT®** slow cooker with cooking spray. Add tomatoes with juice, okra, bell peppers, onion, celery, broth, Worcestershire sauce, thyme and bay leaf. Cover; cook on LOW 9 hours or on HIGH 4½ hours.

2. Coat medium nonstick skillet with cooking spray. Heat over medium-high heat until hot. Add chicken; cook and stir 6 minutes or until beginning to lightly brown. Transfer chicken to **CROCK-POT®** slow cooker. Add remaining ingredients except parsley and cook on HIGH 15 minutes to blend flavors. Stir in parsley.

Makes 8 servings

Nutrition Information: Serving Size about 1½ cups, Calories 209, Total Fat 11g, Saturated Fat 2g, Protein 10g, Carbohydrate 18g, Cholesterol 23mg, Dietary Fiber 3g, Sodium 375mg

Curry Chicken with Mango and Red Pepper

- **6 boneless, skinless chicken thighs or breasts**
- **Salt and black pepper, to taste**
- **Olive oil**
- **1 bag (8 ounces) frozen mango chunks, thawed and drained**
- **2 red bell peppers, cored, seeded and diced**
- **⅓ cup raisins**
- **1 shallot, thinly sliced**
- **¾ cup 99% fat-free chicken broth**
- **1 tablespoon cider vinegar**
- **2 cloves garlic, crushed**
- **4 thin slices fresh ginger**
- **1 teaspoon ground cumin**
- **½ teaspoon curry powder**
- **½ teaspoon whole cloves**
- **¼ teaspoon ground red pepper (optional)**
- **Fresh cilantro (optional)**

1. Rinse, dry and season chicken with salt and pepper.

2. Heat oil in skillet over medium heat until hot. Add chicken and lightly brown, about 3 minutes per side. Transfer to **CROCK-POT®** slow cooker.

3. Add mango, bell peppers, raisins and shallot. Combine remaining ingredients except cilantro in small bowl, and pour over chicken. Cover; cook on LOW 6 to 8 hours or on HIGH 3 to 4 hours.

4. To serve, spoon mangos, raisins and cooking liquid onto chicken. Garnish with cilantro, if desired.

Makes 4 servings

Nutrition Information: Serving Size about 1½ cups, Calories 315, Total Fat 5g, Saturated Fat 1g, Protein 40g, Carbohydrate 26g, Cholesterol 113mg, Dietary Fiber 3g, Sodium 387mg

Quatro Frijoles con Pollo Cantaro

1 **cup pitted black olives, drained**

1 **pound boneless, skinless chicken breasts, cubed**

1 **can (16 ounces) no-salt-added garbanzo beans, rinsed and drained**

1 **can (16 ounces) no-salt-added Great Northern beans, rinsed and drained**

1 **can (15 ounces) no-salt-added cannellini beans, rinsed and drained**

1 **can (16 ounces) no-salt-added red kidney beans, rinsed and drained**

1 **can (7 ounces) chopped mild green chilies, drained**

2 **cups 99% fat-free chicken broth**

1 **tablespoon canola oil**

1 **cup minced yellow onion**

2 **teaspoons minced garlic**

1½ **teaspoons ground cumin**

Hot sauce, to taste

Salt and black pepper, to taste

2 **cups crushed corn chips (optional)**

6 **ounces shredded Monterey Jack cheese (optional)**

1. Combine olives, chicken, beans, chilies and chicken broth in **CROCK-POT®** slow cooker. Mix well; set aside.

2. Heat oil in large skillet over medium-high heat. Cook onion, garlic and cumin until onion is soft, stirring frequently. Add to chicken mixture. Cover; cook on LOW 4 to 5 hours. Check liquid about halfway through, adding more hot water as needed. Add hot sauce, salt and pepper, to taste. Serve in warm bowls garnished with corn chips and cheese, if desired.

Makes 6 servings

Nutrition Information: Serving Size 1½ cups, Calories 417, Total Fat 10g, Saturated Fat 1g, Protein 31g, Carbohydrate 50g, Cholesterol 48mg, Dietary Fiber 14g, Sodium 741mg

Chicken Tangier

     2 **tablespoons dried oregano**

     2 **teaspoons seasoning salt**

     2 **teaspoons puréed garlic**

     ¼ **teaspoon black pepper**

     3 **pounds boneless, skinless chicken breasts**

     1 **lemon, thinly sliced**

     ½ **cup dry white wine**

     2 **tablespoons olive oil**

     1 **cup pitted prunes**

     ¼ **cup raisins**

     ½ **cup pitted green olives**

     2 **tablespoons capers**

        Cooked noodles or rice

        Chopped fresh parsley or cilantro (optional)

> ### Tip
> It may seem like a lot, but this recipe really does call for 2 tablespoons dried oregano in order to more accurately represent the powerfully seasoned flavors of Morocco.

1. Stir together oregano, salt, garlic and pepper in small bowl. Rub onto chicken, being certain to coat all sides.

2. Coat inside of **CROCK-POT**® slow cooker with nonstick cooking spray. Arrange chicken inside, tucking lemon slices between pieces. Pour wine over chicken and sprinkle with olive oil. Add prunes, raisins, olives and capers. Cover and cook on LOW 7 to 8 hours or on HIGH 4 to 5 hours.

3. Serve over cooked noodles or rice and sprinkle with parsley, if desired.

Makes 8 servings

Nutrition Information: Serving Size about 1 cup, Calories 334, Total Fat 10g, Saturated Fat 1g, Protein 37g, Carbohydrate 20g, Cholesterol 109mg, Dietary Fiber 2g, Sodium 742mg

Braised Italian Chicken with Tomatoes and Olives

2 **pounds boneless, skinless chicken breasts**

¼ **teaspoon kosher salt**

½ **teaspoon black pepper**

½ **cup all-purpose flour**

Olive oil

1 **can (14½ ounces) no-salt-added diced tomatoes, drained**

⅓ **cup dry red wine**

⅓ **cup quartered, pitted kalamata olives**

1 **clove garlic, minced**

1 **teaspoon chopped fresh rosemary**

½ **teaspoon red pepper flakes**

Cooked linguini or spaghetti

Grated or shredded Parmesan cheese (optional)

1. Season chicken with salt and pepper. Spread flour on plate, and lightly dredge chicken in flour, coating both sides.

2. Heat oil in skillet over medium heat until hot. Sear chicken in two or three batches until well browned on both sides. Use additional oil as needed to prevent sticking. Transfer to **CROCK-POT®** slow cooker.

3. Add tomatoes, wine, olives and garlic. Cover; cook on LOW 4 to 5 hours.

4. Add rosemary and red pepper flakes; stir in. Cover; cook on LOW 1 hour longer. Serve over linguini. Garnish with cheese, if desired.

Makes 4 servings

Nutrition Information: Serving Size about 1¼ cups, Calories 374, Total Fat 7g, Saturated Fat 1g, Protein 51g, Carbohydrate 18g, Cholesterol 145mg, Dietary Fiber 1g, Sodium 808mg

Poultry Main Dishes

Slow Cooker Turkey Breast

> 1 **turkey breast (3 pounds)**
> **Garlic powder**
> **Paprika**
> **Dried parsley flakes**

1. Place turkey in **CROCK-POT®** slow cooker. Season with garlic powder, paprika and parsley. Cover; cook on LOW 6 to 8 hours or until internal temperature reaches 170°F.

2. Transfer turkey to cutting board; cover with foil and let stand 10 to 15 minutes before carving. (Internal temperature will rise 5° to 10°F during stand time.)

Makes 6 servings

Nutrition Information: Serving Size ⅙ turkey breast, Calories 240, Total Fat 3g, Saturated Fat 1g, Protein 53g, Carbohydrate 0g, Cholesterol 111mg, Dietary Fiber 0g, Sodium 122mg

Italian-Style Turkey Sausage

> 1 **package (about 1 pound) lean Italian turkey sausage, cut into 1-inch pieces**
> 1 **can (about 15 ounces) no-salt-added pinto beans, rinsed and drained**
> 1 **cup low-sodium meatless pasta sauce**
> 1 **medium green bell pepper, cut into strips**
> 1 **small yellow onion, halved and sliced**
> ½ **teaspoon salt**
> ¼ **teaspoon black pepper**
> **Hot cooked rice**
> **Chopped fresh basil (optional)**

1. Brown sausage 6 to 8 minutes in large skillet over medium heat, stirring to break up meat. Drain fat.

2. Add beans, pasta sauce, bell pepper, onion, salt and black pepper to skillet. Cook and stir 20 to 25 minutes until heated through.

3. Serve with rice. Garnish with basil, if desired.

Makes 5 servings

Nutrition Information: Serving Size 1 link sausage and ¼ cup sauce, Calories 202, Total Fat 9g, Saturated Fat 3g, Protein 17g, Carbohydrate 15g, Cholesterol 45mg, Dietary Fiber 4g, Sodium 722mg

**Slow Cooker
Turkey Breast**

Hearty Cassoulet

- 1 **tablespoon olive oil**
- 1 **large yellow onion, finely chopped**
- 1 **pound boneless, skinless chicken breasts, chopped**
- ¼ **pound smoked turkey sausage, finely diced**
- 3 **cloves garlic, minced**
- 1 **teaspoon dried thyme**
- ½ **teaspoon black pepper**
- 4 **tablespoons tomato paste**
- 2 **tablespoons water**
- 3 **cans (about 15 ounces each) Great Northern beans, rinsed and drained**
- ½ **cup dry bread crumbs**
- 3 **tablespoons minced fresh parsley**

Tip

When preparing ingredients for the **CROCK-POT®** slow cooker, cut into uniform pieces so that everything cooks evenly.

1. Heat oil in large skillet over medium heat until hot. Add onion; cook and stir 5 minutes or until onion is tender. Stir in chicken, sausage, garlic, thyme and pepper. Cook 5 minutes or until chicken and sausage are browned.

2. Remove skillet from heat; stir in tomato paste and water until blended. Place beans and chicken mixture in **CROCK-POT®** slow cooker. Cover; cook on LOW 4 to 4½ hours.

3. Before serving, combine bread crumbs and parsley in small bowl. Sprinkle over top of cassoulet.

Makes 8 servings

Nutrition Information: Serving Size about 1 cup, Calories 283, Total Fat 6g, Saturated Fat 1g, Protein 24g, Carbohydrate 31g, Cholesterol 44mg, Dietary Fiber 10g, Sodium 744mg

Forty-Clove Chicken

  1 **whole chicken (3 to 4 pounds), cut up**
     Salt and black pepper
  1 **tablespoon olive oil**
 ¼ **cup dry white wine**
  2 **tablespoons chopped fresh Italian parsley *or* 2 teaspoons dried parsley**
  2 **tablespoons dry vermouth**
  2 **teaspoons dried basil**
  1 **teaspoon dried oregano**
     Pinch red pepper flakes
 40 **cloves garlic (about 2 bulbs), peeled**
  4 **stalks celery, sliced**
     Juice and peel of 1 lemon

1. Remove skin from chicken. Sprinkle chicken with salt and pepper. Heat oil in large skillet over medium heat. Add chicken; brown on all sides. Transfer to platter.

2. Combine wine, parsley, vermouth, basil, oregano and red pepper flakes in large bowl. Add garlic and celery; coat well. Transfer garlic and celery to **CROCK-POT**® slow cooker with slotted spoon.

3. Add chicken to herb mixture; coat well. Place chicken on top of vegetable mixture in **CROCK-POT**® slow cooker; pour any remaining herb mixture over chicken. Sprinkle lemon juice and peel over chicken. Cover; cook on LOW 6 hours.

Makes 6 servings

Nutrition Information: Serving Size ⅙ chicken and sauce, Calories 201, Total Fat 6g, Saturated Fat 1g, Protein 25g, Carbohydrate 9g, Cholesterol 77mg, Dietary Fiber 1g, Sodium 111mg

Turkey Piccata

- 2½ **tablespoons all-purpose flour**
- ¼ **teaspoon salt**
- ¼ **teaspoon black pepper**
- 1 **pound turkey breast, cut into short strips**
- 1 **tablespoon unsalted butter**
- 1 **tablespoon olive oil**
- ½ **cup 99% fat-free chicken broth**
- **Grated peel of 1 lemon**
- 2 **teaspoons lemon juice**
- 2 **tablespoons finely chopped fresh Italian parsley**
- 2 **cups cooked rice (optional)**

1. Combine flour, salt and pepper in resealable food storage bag. Add turkey strips and shake well to coat. Heat butter and oil in large skillet over medium-high heat. Add turkey strips; brown on all sides. Arrange in single layer in **CROCK-POT**® slow cooker.

2. Pour broth into skillet; cook 2 minutes, stirring to scrape up any browned bits. Pour into **CROCK-POT**® slow cooker. Add lemon peel and juice. Cover; cook on LOW 2 hours. Sprinkle with parsley before serving. Serve over rice, if desired.

Makes 4 servings

Nutrition Information: Serving Size about 1¼ cups, Calories 199, Total Fat 8g, Saturated Fat 3g, Protein 27g, Carbohydrate 4g, Cholesterol 63mg, Dietary Fiber 0g, Sodium 386mg

Barley and Sausage Gumbo

- 1 small yellow onion, chopped
- 1 large green bell pepper, chopped
- 1 cup frozen sliced okra
- 1 medium stalk celery, chopped
- 1 clove garlic, minced
- 1 cup reduced-sodium chicken broth
- 1 cup no-salt-added tomato purée
- ¼ cup uncooked pearl barley
- 1 teaspoon dried oregano
- ¼ teaspoon salt (optional)
- ⅛ teaspoon red pepper flakes
- 2 low-fat chicken andouille sausages (3 ounces each), sliced ½ inch thick

1. Place onion, bell pepper, okra, celery and garlic in **CROCK-POT**® slow cooker. Add broth, tomato purée, barley, oregano, salt, if desired, and red pepper flakes; stir. Add sliced sausages. Cover; cook on LOW 5 to 6 hours.

2. Let stand 5 minutes before serving.

Makes 4 servings

Nutrition Information: Serving Size about 1¼ cups, Calories 169, Total Fat 4g, Saturated Fat 1g, Protein 12g, Carbohydrate 23g, Cholesterol 33mg, Dietary Fiber 6g, Sodium 409mg

Spicy Turkey with Citrus Au Jus

- **1 bone-in turkey breast (about 4 pounds)**
- **¼ cup (½ stick) unsalted butter, softened**
- **Grated peel of 1 lemon**
- **1 teaspoon chili powder**
- **¼ to ½ teaspoon black pepper**
- **⅛ to ¼ teaspoon red pepper flakes**
- **1 tablespoon lemon juice**

1. Lightly coat **CROCK-POT**® slow cooker with nonstick cooking spray. Add turkey breast.

2. Mix butter, lemon peel, chili powder, black pepper and red pepper flakes in small bowl until well blended. Spread mixture over top and sides of turkey. Cover; cook on LOW 4 to 5 hours or on HIGH 2½ to 3 hours or until meat thermometer reaches 170°F.

3. Transfer turkey to cutting board. Let stand 10 minutes before slicing.

4. Stir lemon juice into cooking liquid. Strain; discard solids. Let mixture stand 15 minutes. Skim and discard excess fat. Serve au jus with turkey.

Makes 8 servings

Nutrition Information: Serving Size ⅛ turkey breast, Calories 304, Total Fat 7g, Saturated Fat 4g, Protein 56g, Carbohydrate 0g, Cholesterol 156mg, Dietary Fiber 0g, Sodium 115mg

Rice and Chicken Pilaf

- 1 teaspoon olive oil
- 1 medium red bell pepper, cored, seeded and chopped
- 1 celery stalk, trimmed and chopped
- 1 clove garlic, minced
- ½ cup converted rice
- ¼ teaspoon salt
- ⅛ teaspoon black pepper
- ⅛ teaspoon crushed dried thyme
    Dash ground red pepper
- 1 pound boneless, skinless chicken breasts, cut into bite-size pieces
- 1 cup fat-free, reduced-sodium chicken broth
- 1 large green onion, finely chopped (green part only)
- ¼ cup grated Parmesan cheese

1. Heat oil in large nonstick skillet. Add bell pepper, celery and garlic. Cook over medium-high heat 3 to 4 minutes or until vegetables are limp, stirring frequently.

2. Add rice. Cook 1 minute, stirring constantly, until rice is glossy. Stir in salt, black pepper, thyme and red pepper. Spoon into **CROCK-POT®** slow cooker.

3. Add chicken and broth. Stir. Cover; cook on LOW 3½ hours. Stir in green onion. Cover; cook 15 minutes. Sprinkle each serving with 1 tablespoon Parmesan cheese before serving.

Makes 6 servings

Nutrition Information: Serving Size 1 cup, Calories 222, Total Fat 11g, Saturated Fat 4g, Protein 16g, Carbohydrate 14g, Cholesterol 51mg, Dietary Fiber 1g, Sodium 233mg

Tuscan Pasta

- 1 **pound boneless, skinless chicken breasts, cut into 1-inch pieces**
- 2 **cans (about 14 ounces each) Italian-style stewed tomatoes, undrained**
- 1 **can (15 ounces) red kidney beans, rinsed and drained**
- 1 **can (15 ounces) tomato sauce**
- 1 **cup water**
- 1 **jar (4½ ounces) sliced mushrooms, drained**
- 1 **medium green bell pepper, chopped**
- ½ **cup chopped yellow onion**
- ½ **cup chopped celery**
- 4 **cloves garlic, minced**
- 1 **teaspoon Italian seasoning**
- 6 **ounces uncooked thin spaghetti, broken in half**

1. Place all ingredients except spaghetti in **CROCK-POT®** slow cooker.

2. Cover; cook on LOW 4 hours or until vegetables are tender.

3. Stir in spaghetti. Cook on HIGH 10 minutes; stir. Cover; cook 35 minutes or until pasta is tender.

Makes 8 servings

Nutrition Information: Serving Size about 1½ cups, Calories 408, Total Fat 7g, Saturated Fat 2g, Protein 28g, Carbohydrate 60g, Cholesterol 36mg, Dietary Fiber 16g, Sodium 565mg

Turkey Ropa Vieja

- **12 ounces turkey tenderloin (2 large or 3 small) or boneless, skinless chicken thighs**
- **1 can (8 ounces) no-salt-added tomato sauce**
- **2 medium tomatoes, chopped**
- **1 small yellow onion, thinly sliced**
- **1 small green bell pepper, chopped**
- **4 pimiento-stuffed green olives, sliced**
- **1 clove garlic, minced**
- **¾ teaspoon ground cumin**
- **½ teaspoon dried oregano**
- **⅛ teaspoon black pepper**
- **2 teaspoons lemon juice**
- **¼ teaspoon salt (optional)**
- **1 cup cooked brown rice (optional)**
- **1 cup cooked black beans (optional)**

1. Place turkey in **CROCK-POT®** slow cooker. Add tomato sauce, tomatoes, onion, bell pepper, olives, garlic, cumin, oregano and black pepper. Cover; cook on LOW 6 to 7 hours.

2. Shred turkey using 2 forks. Stir in lemon juice and salt, if desired. Serve with rice and black beans, if desired.

Makes 4 servings

Nutrition Information: Serving Size about 1½ cups, Calories 146, Total Fat 2g, Saturated Fat 0g, Protein 22g, Carbohydrate 11g, Cholesterol 42mg, Dietary Fiber 2g, Sodium 182mg

Autumn Herbed Chicken with Fennel and Squash

- 3 **pounds boneless, skinless chicken breasts**
- **Salt and black pepper, to taste**
- **All-purpose flour, as needed**
- 2 **tablespoons olive oil**
- 1 **fennel bulb, thinly sliced**
- ½ **butternut squash, peeled, seeded and cut into ¾-inch cubes**
- 1 **teaspoon dried thyme**
- ¾ **cup walnuts (optional)**
- ¾ **cup 99% fat-free chicken broth**
- ½ **cup unsweetened apple juice**
- **Cooked rice or pasta**
- ¼ **cup fresh basil, sliced into ribbons**
- 2 **teaspoons fresh rosemary, finely minced**

1. Season chicken on all sides with salt and pepper, then lightly coat with flour. Heat oil in skillet over medium heat until hot. Brown chicken in batches to prevent crowding. Brown on each side 3 to 5 minutes, turning once. Remove with slotted spoon. Transfer to **CROCK-POT®** slow cooker.

2. Add fennel, squash and thyme. Stir well to combine. Add walnuts, if desired, broth and juice. Cover; cook on LOW 5 to 7 hours or on HIGH 2½ to 4½ hours.

3. Serve over rice or pasta and garnish with basil and fresh rosemary.

Makes 6 servings

Nutrition Information: Serving Size makes about 1¼ cups, Calories 356, Total Fat 11g, Saturated Fat 2g, Protein 50g, Carbohydrate 14g, Cholesterol 145mg, Dietary Fiber 3g, Sodium 403mg

Mediterranean Chicken

- 1 tablespoon olive oil
- 2 pounds boneless, skinless chicken breasts
  Juice of 2 lemons
- 2 cinnamon sticks
- 6 teaspoons minced garlic
- 1 can (28 ounces) diced tomatoes, undrained
- 1 bay leaf
- ½ teaspoon black pepper
- ½ cup sherry
- 2 medium yellow onions, chopped
- 1 pound cooked broad noodles
- ½ cup feta cheese

1. Heat oil in large skillet. Add the chicken and lightly brown.

2. Combine lemon juice, cinnamon, garlic, tomatoes with juice, bay leaf, pepper, sherry and onions in the **CROCK-POT®** slow cooker. Add chicken. Cover; cook on LOW 8 to 10 hours or on HIGH 4 to 5 hours or until done.

3. Discard cinnamon sticks and bay leaf. Serve chicken and sauce over cooked noodles. Sprinkle with cheese just before serving.

Makes 8 servings

Nutrition Information: Serving Size about 1½ cups, Calories 432, Total Fat 8g, Saturated Fat 3g, Protein 34g, Carbohydrate 51g, Cholesterol 81mg, Dietary Fiber 3g, Sodium 440mg

Turkey Breast with Barley-Cranberry Stuffing

1 **fresh or thawed frozen bone-in turkey breast half (about 2 pounds), skinned**

2 **cups reduced-sodium chicken broth**

1 **cup uncooked quick-cooking barley**

½ **cup chopped yellow onion**

½ **cup dried cranberries**

2 **tablespoons slivered almonds, toasted***

½ **teaspoon rubbed sage**

½ **teaspoon garlic-pepper seasoning**

⅓ **cup finely chopped fresh parsley**

To toast almonds, spread in single layer on baking sheet. Bake in preheated 350°F oven 8 to 10 minutes or until golden brown, stirring frequently.

1. Thaw turkey breast, if frozen. Remove skin and discard.

2. Combine broth, barley, onion, cranberries, almonds, sage and garlic-pepper seasoning in **CROCK-POT®** slow cooker.

3. Coat large nonstick skillet with cooking spray. Heat over medium heat until hot. Brown turkey breast on all sides; add to **CROCK-POT®** slow cooker. Cover; cook on LOW 4 to 6 hours.

4. Transfer turkey to cutting board; cover with foil to keep warm. Let stand 10 to 15 minutes before carving. Stir parsley into sauce mixture in **CROCK-POT®** slow cooker. Serve over sliced turkey and stuffing.

Makes 6 servings

Nutrition Information: Serving Size ⅙ turkey breast, Calories 379, Total Fat 12g, Saturated Fat 3g, Protein 35g, Carbohydrate 33g, Cholesterol 88mg, Dietary Fiber 7g, Sodium 306mg

Simple Coq au Vin

 1 **pound boneless, skinless chicken breasts**
    Salt and black pepper
 2 **tablespoons olive oil**
 8 **ounces mushrooms, sliced**
 1 **medium yellow onion, cut into rings**
 ½ **cup red wine**
 ½ **teaspoon dried basil**
 ½ **teaspoon dried thyme**
 ½ **teaspoon dried oregano**
    Hot cooked rice (optional)

Tip

Browning poultry before cooking it in the **CROCK-POT®** slow cooker isn't necessary but helps to enhance the flavor and adds an oven-roasted appearance to the finished dish.

1. Sprinkle chicken with salt and pepper. Heat oil in large skillet over medium-high heat; brown chicken on all sides. Transfer chicken to **CROCK-POT®** slow cooker.

2. Cook and stir mushrooms and onion in same skillet 5 minutes or until tender. Add wine; stir and scrape brown bits from bottom of skillet. Add mixture to **CROCK-POT®** slow cooker. Sprinkle with basil, thyme and oregano. Cover; cook on LOW 8 to 10 hours or on HIGH 3 to 4 hours. Serve over rice, if desired.

Makes 4 servings

Nutrition Information: Serving Size about 1 cup chicken and sauce, Calories 245, Total Fat 11g, Saturated Fat 2g, Protein 25g, Carbohydrate 6g, Cholesterol 72mg, Dietary Fiber 1g, Sodium 138mg

Herbed Artichoke Chicken

1½ pounds boneless, skinless chicken breasts

1 can (14 ounces) no-salt-added tomatoes, drained and diced

1 can (14 ounces) artichoke hearts in water, drained

1 small yellow onion, chopped

½ cup kalamata olives, pitted and sliced

1 cup 99% fat-free, reduced-sodium chicken broth

¼ cup dry white wine

3 tablespoons quick-cooking tapioca

2 teaspoons curry powder

1 tablespoon chopped fresh Italian parsley

1 teaspoon dried sweet basil

1 teaspoon dried thyme leaves

½ teaspoon salt

½ teaspoon freshly ground black pepper

Note

Inviting flavors of tomato, artichokes, Greek olives and herbs imbue the chicken and tease the appetite!

1. Combine chicken, tomatoes, artichokes, onion, olives, broth, wine, tapioca, curry powder, parsley, basil, thyme, salt and pepper in the **CROCK-POT®** slow cooker. Mix thoroughly.

2. Cover; cook on LOW 6 to 8 hours or on HIGH 3½ to 4 hours or until chicken is no longer pink in center.

Makes 8 servings

Nutrition Information: Serving Size about 1½ cups, Calories 219, Total Fat 11g, Saturated Fat 3g, Protein 18g, Carbohydrate 13g, Cholesterol 54mg, Dietary Fiber 3g, Sodium 569mg

Fusilli Pizzaiola with Turkey Meatballs

- 2 cans (about 14 ounces each) no-salt-added whole tomatoes
- 1 can (8 ounces) no-salt-added tomato sauce
- ¼ cup chopped yellow onion
- ¼ cup grated carrot
- 2 tablespoons no-salt-added tomato paste
- 2 tablespoons chopped fresh basil
- 1 clove garlic, minced
- ½ teaspoon dried thyme leaves
- ¼ teaspoon sugar
- ¼ teaspoon black pepper, divided
- 1 bay leaf
- 1 pound 93% lean ground turkey breast
- 1 egg, lightly beaten
- 1 tablespoon fat-free (skim) milk
- ¼ cup Italian-seasoned dry bread crumbs
- 2 tablespoons chopped parsley
- 8 ounces uncooked fusilli or other spiral-shaped pasta

1. Combine tomatoes, tomato sauce, onion, carrot, basil, tomato paste, garlic, thyme, sugar, ⅛ teaspoon pepper and bay leaf in **CROCK-POT®** slow cooker. Break up tomatoes gently with wooden spoon. Cover; cook on LOW 4½ to 5 hours.

2. About 45 minutes before end of cooking, prepare meatballs. Preheat oven to 350°F. Combine turkey, egg and milk; blend in bread crumbs, parsley and remaining ⅛ teaspoon pepper. With wet hands, shape mixture into small balls. Spray baking sheet with nonstick cooking spray. Arrange meatballs on baking sheet; bake 25 minutes or until no longer pink in center.

3. Add meatballs to **CROCK-POT®** slow cooker. Cover; cook 45 minutes to 1 hour or until meatballs are heated through. Remove and discard bay leaf. Prepare pasta according to package directions; drain. Place pasta in serving bowl; top with meatballs and sauce.

Makes 4 servings

Nutrition Information: Serving Size about 1½ cups, Calories 479, Total Fat 10g, Saturated Fat 3g, Protein 35g, Carbohydrate 65g, Cholesterol 119mg, Dietary Fiber 6g, Sodium 273mg

Vegetarian Main Dishes

Ziti Ratatouille

- **1 large eggplant, peeled and cut into ½-inch cubes (about 1½ pounds)**
- **2 medium zucchini, cut into ½-inch cubes**
- **1 green or red bell pepper, seeded and cut into ½-inch pieces**
- **1 large yellow onion, chopped**
- **4 cloves garlic, minced**
- **1 jar (about 24 ounces) marinara sauce**
- **2 cans (about 14 ounces each) diced tomatoes with garlic and onions, undrained**
- **1 can (6 ounces) pitted black olives, drained**
- **1 package (8 ounces) ziti noodles**
- **Lemon juice (optional)**
- **Shredded Parmesan cheese (optional)**

1. Combine eggplant, zucchini, bell pepper, onion, garlic, marinara sauce and tomatoes with juice in **CROCK-POT®** slow cooker. Cover and cook on LOW 4½ hours.

2. Stir in olives and pasta and cook 25 minutes more. Drizzle with lemon juice and sprinkle with Parmesan cheese, if desired.

Makes 8 servings

Nutrition Information: Serving Size about 1½ cups, Calories 275, Total Fat 7g, Saturated Fat 1g, Protein 8g, Carbohydrate 47g, Cholesterol 2mg, Dietary Fiber 7g, Sodium 692mg

Vegetarian Main Dishes

Bean and Vegetable Burritos

- 2 **tablespoons chili powder**
- 2 **teaspoons dried oregano**
- 1½ **teaspoons ground cumin**
- 1 **large sweet potato, peeled and diced**
- 1 **can (15 ounces) black beans, rinsed and drained**
- 4 **cloves garlic, minced**
- 1 **medium yellow onion, halved and thinly sliced**
- 1 **jalapeño pepper, seeded and minced***
- 1 **green bell pepper, chopped**
- 1 **cup frozen corn, thawed and drained**
- 3 **tablespoons lime juice**
- 1 **tablespoon chopped fresh cilantro**
- ¾ **cup (3 ounces) shredded Monterey Jack cheese**
- 6 **(10-inch) flour tortillas**

Jalapeño peppers can sting and irritate the skin, so wear rubber gloves when handling peppers and do not touch your eyes.

1. Combine chili powder, oregano and cumin in small bowl. Set aside.

2. Layer ingredients in **CROCK-POT®** slow cooker in following order: sweet potato, beans, half of chili powder mixture, garlic, onion, jalapeño pepper, bell pepper, remaining half of chili powder mixture and corn. Cover; cook on LOW 5 hours or until sweet potato is tender. Stir in lime juice and cilantro.

3. Preheat oven to 350°F. Spoon 2 tablespoons cheese into center of each tortilla. Top with 1 cup filling. Fold up bottom edge of tortilla over filling; fold in sides and roll to enclose filling. Place burrito, seam side down, on baking sheet. Repeat with remaining tortillas. Cover with foil and bake 20 to 30 minutes or until heated through.

Makes 6 servings

Nutrition Information: Serving Size 1 burrito, Calories 392, Total Fat 11g, Saturated Fat 4g, Protein 14g, Carbohydrate 60g, Cholesterol 15mg, Dietary Fiber 8g, Sodium 800mg

Italian Escarole and White Bean Stew

1 **tablespoon olive oil**

1 **medium yellow onion, chopped**

3 **medium carrots, cut into ½-inch-thick rounds**

2 **cloves garlic, minced**

1 **can (14½ ounces each) vegetable broth**

1 **head (about 12 ounces) escarole**

¼ **teaspoon red pepper flakes**

2 **cans (15½ ounces each) Great Northern beans, rinsed and drained**

Salt

Grated Parmesan cheese (optional)

> ## Tip
> Escarole is very leafy and easily fills a 4½-quart **CROCK-POT®** slow cooker when raw, but it shrinks dramatically as it cooks down. This recipe makes 4 portions, but can easily be doubled. Simply double the quantities of all the ingredients listed and be sure to use a 6-quart (or larger) **CROCK-POT®** slow cooker.

1. Heat oil in medium skillet over medium-high heat. Add onion and carrots. Cook, stirring occasionally, until onion softens. Add garlic and stir until fragrant, about 1 minute. Transfer to **CROCK-POT®** slow cooker. Top with vegetable broth.

2. Trim off base of escarole. Roughly cut crosswise into 1-inch-wide strips. Wash well in large bowl of cold water. Lift out by handfuls, leaving sand or dirt in bottom of bowl. Shake to remove excess water, but do not dry. Add to vegetable mixture in **CROCK-POT®** slow cooker. Sprinkle with red pepper flakes. Top with beans.

3. Cover; cook on LOW 7 to 8 hours or on HIGH 3½ to 4 hours, until escarole is wilted and very tender. Season with salt. Serve in bowls and sprinkle with Parmesan cheese, if desired.

Makes 4 servings

Nutrition Information: Serving Size about 1½ cups, Calories 336, Total Fat 5g, Saturated Fat 1g, Protein 18g, Carbohydrate 58g, Cholesterol 0mg, Dietary Fiber 15g, Sodium 474mg

Vegetarian Main Dishes

Curried Potatoes, Cauliflower and Peas

1 **tablespoon vegetable oil**

1 **large yellow onion, chopped**

2 **tablespoons peeled and minced fresh ginger**

2 **cloves garlic, chopped**

2 **pounds red-skinned potatoes, scrubbed, cut into ½-inch-thick rounds**

1 **teaspoon garam masala***

1 **teaspoon salt, plus more to taste**

1 **small (about 1¼ pounds) head cauliflower, trimmed and broken into florets**

1 **cup vegetable broth**

2 **ripe plum (Roma) tomatoes, seeded and chopped**

1 **cup thawed frozen peas**

Hot cooked basmati or long-grain rice

*Garam masala is a blend of Asian spices available in the spice aisle of many supermarkets. If garam masala is unavailable substitute ½ teaspoon ground cumin and ½ teaspoon ground coriander seeds.

1. Heat oil in large skillet over medium heat. Add onion, ginger and garlic. Cook, stirring occasionally, until onion softens. Remove from heat and set aside.

2. Put potatoes in **CROCK-POT®** slow cooker. Mix garam masala and salt in small bowl. Sprinkle half of spice mixture over potatoes. Top with onion mixture, then cauliflower. Sprinkle remaining spice mixture over cauliflower. Pour in broth. Cover; cook on HIGH 3½ hours.

3. Remove cover and gently stir in tomatoes and peas. Cover and cook for 30 minutes more or until potatoes are tender. Stir gently. Adjust seasoning with more salt, if desired. Spoon over rice in bowls and serve.

Makes 6 servings

Nutrition Information: Serving Size about 1 cup, Calories 174, Total Fat 3g, Saturated Fat 0g, Protein 6g, Carbohydrate 34g, Cholesterol 0mg, Dietary Fiber 5g, Sodium 569mg

Vegetarian Main Dishes

Black Bean and Mushroom Chilaquiles

   2 **tablespoons olive oil**

   1 **medium yellow onion, chopped**

   1 **medium green bell pepper, seeded and ribbed, chopped**

   1 **jalapeño pepper, seeded and minced***

   2 **cans (about 15 ounces each) black beans, drained and rinsed**

   1 **can (14½ ounces) diced tomatoes, undrained**

 10 **ounces white mushrooms, cut into quarters**

1½ **teaspoons ground cumin**

1½ **teaspoons dried oregano**

   1 **cup (about 2 ounces) shredded sharp white Cheddar cheese, plus additional cheese for garnish**

   6 **cups baked tortilla chips**

*Jalapeño peppers can sting and irritate the skin, so wear rubber gloves when handling peppers and do not touch your eyes.

1. Heat oil in medium skillet over medium heat. Add onion, bell pepper and minced jalapeño. Cook, stirring occasionally, until onion softens. Transfer to **CROCK-POT**® slow cooker. Add beans, tomatoes with juice, mushrooms, cumin and oregano. Cover; cook on LOW 6 hours or on HIGH 3 hours.

2. Remove cover and sprinkle Cheddar cheese over beans and mushrooms. Cover again and cook until cheese melts; stir to combine melted cheese.

3. For each serving, coarsely crush 1 cup tortilla chips in individual serving bowl. Top with black bean mixture, sprinkle with additional cheese, if desired, and serve.

Makes 6 servings

Nutrition Information: Serving Size about 1½ cups, Calories 347, Total Fat 11g, Saturated Fat 3g, Protein 14g, Carbohydrate 49g, Cholesterol 10mg, Dietary Fiber 9g, Sodium 755mg

Vegetarian Main Dishes

Bean Ragoût with Cilantro-Cornmeal Dumplings

2 **cans (about 14 ounces each) diced tomatoes**

1 **can (about 15 ounces) no-salt-added pinto beans, rinsed and drained**

1 **can (about 15 ounces) no-salt-added black beans, rinsed and drained**

1½ **cups chopped red bell peppers**

1 **large yellow onion, chopped**

2 **small zucchini, sliced**

½ **cup chopped green bell pepper**

½ **cup chopped celery**

1 **poblano pepper, seeded and chopped***

2 **cloves garlic, minced**

3 **tablespoons chili powder**

2 **teaspoons ground cumin**

1 **teaspoon dried oregano**

¼ **teaspoon salt**

⅛ **teaspoon black pepper**

Cilantro-Cornmeal Dumplings (recipe follows)

Poblano peppers can sting and irritate the skin, so wear rubber gloves when handling peppers and do not touch your eyes.

1. Combine tomatoes, beans, red bell peppers, onion, zucchini, green bell pepper, celery, poblano pepper, garlic, chili powder, cumin, oregano, salt and black pepper in **CROCK-POT®** slow cooker; mix well. Cover; cook on LOW 7 to 8 hours.

2. Prepare dumpling dough 1 hour before serving. Turn **CROCK-POT®** slow cooker to HIGH. Drop dumplings by level tablespoonfuls (larger dumplings will not cook properly) on top of ragoût. Cover; cook 1 hour or until toothpick inserted into dumplings comes out clean.

Makes 6 servings

Nutrition Information: Serving Size about 2 cups ragoût and 3 dumplings, Calories 256, Total Fat 4g, Saturated Fat 1g, Protein 12g, Carbohydrate 44g, Cholesterol 2mg, Dietary Fiber 12g, Sodium 721mg

**Bean Ragoût with
Cilantro-Cornmeal
Dumplings**

Cilantro-Cornmeal Dumplings

- ¼ **cup all-purpose flour**
- ¼ **cup yellow cornmeal**
- ½ **teaspoon baking powder**
- ¼ **teaspoon salt**
- 1 **tablespoon shortening**
- 1 **tablespoon shredded Cheddar cheese**
- 2 **teaspoons minced fresh cilantro**
- ¼ **cup 2% milk**

Mix flour, cornmeal, baking powder and salt in medium bowl. Cut in shortening with pastry blender or two knives until mixture resembles coarse crumbs. Stir in cheese and cilantro. Pour milk into flour mixture. Stir just until dry ingredients are moistened.

Vegetable Curry

- **4 baking potatoes, diced**
- **1 large yellow onion, chopped**
- **1 red bell pepper, chopped**
- **2 carrots, diced**
- **2 tomatoes, chopped**
- **1 can (6 ounces) tomato paste**
- **¾ cup water**
- **2 teaspoons cumin seeds**
- **½ teaspoon garlic powder**
- **½ teaspoon salt**
- **3 cups cauliflower**
- **1 package (10 ounces) frozen peas, thawed**

Combine potatoes, onion, bell pepper, carrots and tomatoes in **CROCK-POT®** slow cooker. Stir in tomato paste, water, cumin seeds, garlic powder and salt. Add cauliflower; stir well. Cover; cook on LOW 8 to 9 hours or until vegetables are tender. Stir in peas before serving.

Makes 6 servings

Nutrition Information: Serving Size about 1½ cups, Calories 191, Total Fat 1g, Saturated Fat 0g, Protein 7g, Carbohydrate 41g, Cholesterol 0mg, Dietary Fiber 9g, Sodium 464mg

Vegetarian Paella

- 2 **tablespoons olive oil**
- 1 **medium yellow onion, chopped**
- 1 **medium red bell pepper, seeded and ribbed, chopped**
- 2 **cloves garlic, minced**
- 1½ **cups uncooked converted rice**
- 2 **cans (14½ ounces each) reduced-sodium vegetable broth**
- ½ **cup dry white wine**
- ½ **teaspoon crushed saffron threads, smoked paprika or ground turmeric**
- ¾ **teaspoon salt**
- ¼ **teaspoon red pepper flakes**
- 1 **can (about 15 ounces) garbanzo beans, rinsed and drained**
- 1 **package (11 ounces) frozen artichoke hearts, thawed**
- ½ **cup frozen peas, thawed**

1. Heat oil in medium skillet over medium heat. Add onion, bell pepper and garlic. Cook, stirring occasionally, until onion softens. Transfer to **CROCK-POT®** slow cooker. Add rice, broth, wine, saffron, salt and red pepper flakes. Stir to level rice. Cover; cook on LOW 3 hours.

2. Add garbanzo beans, artichoke hearts and peas to **CROCK-POT®** slow cooker; do not stir. Cover and cook on LOW about 30 minutes, until rice is tender and liquid is absorbed. Stir well and serve hot.

Makes 6 servings

Nutrition Information: Serving Size about 2 cups, Calories 375, Total Fat 7g, Saturated Fat 1g, Protein 9g, Carbohydrate 65g, Cholesterol 0mg, Dietary Fiber 8g, Sodium 634mg

Caribbean Sweet Potato and Bean Stew

2 medium sweet potatoes (about 1 pound), peeled and cut into 1-inch cubes

2 cups frozen cut green beans

1 can (15 ounces) black beans, rinsed and drained

1 can (14½ ounces) reduced-sodium vegetable broth

1 small yellow onion, sliced

2 teaspoons Caribbean jerk seasoning

½ teaspoon dried thyme

¼ teaspoon salt

¼ teaspoon ground cinnamon

⅓ cup slivered almonds, toasted*

To toast almonds, spread in single layer on baking sheet. Bake in preheated 350°F oven 8 to 10 minutes or until golden brown, stirring frequently.

Combine sweet potatoes, beans, broth, onion, jerk seasoning, thyme, salt and cinnamon in **CROCK-POT®** slow cooker. Cover; cook on LOW 5 to 6 hours or until vegetables are tender. Adjust seasonings. Serve with almonds.

Makes 4 servings

Nutrition Information: Serving Size about 2 cups, Calories 221, Total Fat 5g, Saturated Fat 0g, Protein 9g, Carbohydrate 34g, Cholesterol 0mg, Dietary Fiber 9g, Sodium 708mg

Ratatouille with Garbanzo Beans

- **3** **tablespoons olive oil, divided**
- **4** **cloves garlic, minced**
- **1** **yellow onion, cut into ½-inch dice**
- **4** **small Italian eggplants, peeled and cut into ¾- to 1-inch dice**
  Salt and black pepper, to taste
- **1** **red bell pepper, seeded and cut into ¾- to 1-inch dice**
- **1** **yellow bell pepper, seeded and cut into ¾- to 1-inch dice**
- **1** **orange bell pepper, seeded and cut into ¾- to 1-inch dice**
- **3** **small zucchini, cut into ¾-inch dice**
- **1** **can (15 to 20 ounces) garbanzo beans, rinsed and drained**
- **2** **cups crushed tomatoes**
- **¼** **cup fresh basil**
- **2** **tablespoons chopped fresh thyme**
- **½** **to 1 teaspoon crushed red pepper flakes**
  Fresh basil for garnish (optional)

1. Heat 1 tablespoon oil in skillet on medium-low until hot. Add garlic and onion, and cook 2 to 3 minutes or until translucent. Add eggplants, season with salt and black pepper and cook 1 to 2 minutes. Turn heat to low and cover. Cook 4 to 5 minutes, or until eggplants are tender. Transfer to **CROCK-POT®** slow cooker.

2. Add bell peppers, zucchini and garbanzo beans.

3. Combine tomatoes, basil, thyme, red pepper flakes and remaining 2 tablespoons oil in medium bowl; stir well. Pour into **CROCK-POT®** slow cooker. Stir together all ingredients.

4. Cover; cook on LOW 7 to 8 hours or on HIGH 4½ to 5 hours, or until vegetables are tender. Adjust seasonings. Garnish with fresh basil, if desired.

Makes 8 servings

Nutrition Information: Serving Size about 1½ cups, Calories 190, Total Fat 7g, Saturated Fat 1g, Protein 6g, Carbohydrate 29g, Cholesterol 0mg, Dietary Fiber 8g, Sodium 257mg

Hearty Lentil Stew

1   **cup dried lentils, rinsed and sorted**

1   **package (16 ounces) frozen green beans, thawed**

2   **cups cauliflower florets**

1   **cup chopped yellow onion**

1   **cup baby carrots, cut into halves crosswise**

3   **cups fat-free, reduced-sodium chicken broth**

2   **teaspoons ground cumin**

¾   **teaspoon ground ginger**

1   **can (15 ounces) chunky tomato sauce with garlic and herbs**

½   **cup dry-roasted peanuts**

1. Place lentils in **CROCK-POT®** slow cooker. Top with green beans, cauliflower, onion and carrots.

2. Combine broth, cumin and ginger in large bowl; mix well. Pour over vegetables in **CROCK-POT®** slow cooker. Cover; cook on LOW 9 to 11 hours.

3. Stir in tomato sauce. Cover; cook on LOW 10 minutes. Ladle stew into bowls. Sprinkle peanuts evenly over each serving.

Makes 6 servings

Nutrition Information: Serving Size about 1½ cups, Calories 265, Total Fat 7g, Saturated Fat 1g, Protein 15g, Carbohydrate 39g, Cholesterol 0mg, Dietary Fiber 15g, Sodium 504mg

Spinach and Ricotta Stuffed Shells

- 1 package (16 ounces) jumbo pasta shells
- 1 package (15 ounces) reduced-fat ricotta cheese
- 7 ounces frozen chopped spinach, thawed and squeezed dry
- ½ cup grated reduced-fat Parmesan cheese
- 1 egg, lightly beaten
- 1 clove garlic, minced
- ½ teaspoon salt
- 1 jar (26 ounces) marinara sauce
- ½ cup (2 ounces) shredded reduced-fat mozzarella cheese
- 1 teaspoon olive oil

1. Cook pasta shells according to package directions until almost tender. Drain well; set aside. Stir together ricotta cheese, spinach, Parmesan cheese, egg, garlic and salt. Set aside.

2. Pour ¼ cup marinara sauce in bottom of **CROCK-POT**® slow cooker. Spoon 2 to 3 tablespoons ricotta mixture into 1 pasta shell and place in bottom of **CROCK-POT**® slow cooker. Repeat with enough additional shells to cover bottom of **CROCK-POT**® slow cooker. Top with another ¼ cup marinara sauce. Repeat with remaining pasta shells and filling. Top with any remaining marinara sauce and sprinkle with mozzarella cheese. Drizzle with oil.

3. Cover and cook on HIGH 3 to 4 hours or until mozzarella cheese is melted and sauce is hot and bubbly.

Makes 6 servings

Nutrition Information: Serving Size about 3 shells, Calories 385, Total Fat 8g, Saturated Fat 4g, Protein 18g, Carbohydrate 59g, Cholesterol 50mg, Dietary Fiber 5g, Sodium 727mg

Vegetarian Main Dishes

Southwestern Stuffed Peppers

 4 green bell peppers

 1 can (15 ounces) black beans, rinsed and drained

 1 cup (4 ounces) shredded pepper jack cheese

 ¾ cup medium salsa

 ½ cup frozen corn

 ½ cup chopped green onions with tops

 ⅓ cup uncooked long-grain white rice

 1 teaspoon chili powder

 ½ teaspoon ground cumin

     Sour cream (optional)

Tip

If you prefer firmer rice, substitute converted rice for regular long-grain white rice.

1. Cut thin slice off top of each bell pepper. Carefully remove seeds and membrane, leaving pepper whole.

2. Combine beans, cheese, salsa, corn, onions, rice, chili powder and cumin in medium bowl. Spoon filling evenly into each pepper. Place peppers in **CROCK-POT®** slow cooker.

3. Cover; cook on LOW 4 to 6 hours. Serve with sour cream, if desired.

Makes 4 servings

Nutrition Information: Serving Size 1 stuffed pepper, Calories 323, Total Fat 10g, Saturated Fat 3g, Protein 15g, Carbohydrate 43g, Cholesterol 30mg, Dietary Fiber 7g, Sodium 796mg

Vegetarian Sausage Rice

- 2 **cups chopped green bell peppers**
- 1 **can (15 ounces) no-salt-added dark kidney beans, drained and rinsed**
- 1 **can (14½ ounces) diced tomatoes with green bell peppers and onions, undrained**
- 1 **cup chopped yellow onion**
- 1 **cup sliced celery**
- 1 **cup water, divided**
- ¾ **cup uncooked converted long-grain rice**
- 1¼ **teaspoons salt**
- 1 **teaspoon hot pepper sauce, plus additional for garnish**
- ½ **teaspoon dried thyme**
- ½ **teaspoon red pepper flakes**
- 3 **bay leaves**
- 1 **package (8 ounces) vegetable-protein breakfast patties, thawed**
- 2 **tablespoons extra-virgin olive oil**
- ½ **cup chopped fresh parsley**

1. Combine bell peppers, beans, tomatoes with juice, onion, celery, ½ cup water, rice, salt, hot sauce, thyme, pepper flakes and bay leaves in **CROCK-POT®** slow cooker. Cover; cook on LOW 4 to 5 hours. Remove and discard bay leaves.

2. Dice breakfast patties. Heat oil in large nonstick skillet over medium-high heat until hot. Add patties; cook 2 minutes or until lightly browned, scraping bottom of skillet occasionally.

3. Place patties in **CROCK-POT®** slow cooker. Do not stir. Add remaining ½ cup water to skillet; bring to a boil over high heat 1 minute, scraping up browned bits on bottom of skillet. Add liquid and parsley to **CROCK-POT®** slow cooker; stir gently to blend. Serve immediately with additional hot sauce, if desired.

Makes 8 servings

Nutrition Information: Serving Size about 1¼ cups, Calories 198, Total Fat 5g, Saturated Fat 1g, Protein 11g, Carbohydrate 30g, Cholesterol 0mg, Dietary Fiber 7g, Sodium 715mg

Vegetarian Main Dishes

Broccoli and Cheese Strata

- **2 cups chopped broccoli florets**
- **4 slices firm white bread, ½ inch thick**
- **1 tablespoon unsalted butter**
- **1 cup (4 ounces) shredded Cheddar cheese**
- **1½ cups low-fat (1%) milk**
- **2 eggs**
- **2 egg whites**
- **½ teaspoon salt**
- **½ teaspoon hot pepper sauce**
- **⅛ teaspoon black pepper**

1. Lightly coat 1-quart casserole or soufflé dish that will fit inside your **CROCK-POT®** slow cooker with nonstick cooking spray. Cook broccoli in boiling water 10 minutes or until tender. Drain. Spread one side of each bread slice with butter. Arrange 2 slices bread, buttered sides up, in prepared casserole dish. Layer cheese, broccoli and remaining 2 bread slices, buttered sides down.

2. Beat milk, eggs, egg whites, salt, hot pepper sauce and black pepper in medium bowl. Slowly pour over bread.

3. Place small wire rack in **CROCK-POT®** slow cooker. Pour in 1 cup water. Place casserole on rack. Cover; cook on HIGH 3 hours.

Makes 4 servings

Nutrition Information: Serving Size ¼ strata, Calories 201, Total Fat 8g, Saturated Fat 4g, Protein 13g, Carbohydrate 20g, Cholesterol 91mg, Dietary Fiber 1g, Sodium 618mg

Corn Bread and Bean Casserole

Filling

- 1 **medium yellow onion, chopped**
- 1 **medium green bell pepper, diced**
- 2 **cloves garlic, minced**
- 1 **can (16 ounces) no-salt-added red kidney beans, rinsed and drained**
- 1 **can (16 ounces) no-salt-added pinto beans, rinsed and drained**
- 1 **can (16 ounces) no-salt-added diced tomatoes, undrained**
- 1 **can (8 ounces) no-salt-added tomato sauce**
- 1 **teaspoon chili powder**
- ½ **teaspoon ground cumin**
- ½ **teaspoon black pepper**
- ¼ **teaspoon hot pepper sauce**

Topping

- 1 **cup yellow cornmeal**
- 1 **cup all-purpose flour**
- 2½ **teaspoons baking powder**
- 1 **tablespoon sugar**
- ½ **teaspoon salt**
- 1¼ **cups 2% milk**
- 2 **eggs**
- 3 **tablespoons vegetable oil**
- 1 **can (8½ ounces) cream-style corn, undrained**

1. Spray **CROCK-POT®** slow cooker with nonstick cooking spray. For filling, cook onion, bell pepper and garlic in large skillet over medium heat until tender. Transfer to **CROCK-POT®** slow cooker.

2. Stir in beans, tomatoes with juice, tomato sauce, chili powder, cumin, black pepper and hot sauce. Cover; cook on HIGH 1 hour.

3. For topping, combine cornmeal, flour, baking powder, sugar and salt in large bowl. Stir in milk, eggs and oil; mix well. Stir in corn. Spoon evenly over bean mixture in **CROCK-POT®** slow cooker. Cover; cook on HIGH 1½ to 2 hours or until corn bread topping is done.

Makes 8 servings

Nutrition Information: Serving Size about 1½ cups, Calories 356, Total Fat 8g, Saturated Fat 1g, Protein 14g, Carbohydrate 58g, Cholesterol 57mg, Dietary Fiber 10g, Sodium 660mg

Vegetarian Main Dishes

Slow-Cooked Summer Vegetable Stew

- 1 **cup reduced-sodium vegetable broth**
- 1 **can (15½ ounces) chickpeas, drained**
- 2 **medium zucchini or summer squash, or a combination of the two, cut into ½-inch chunks**
- 4 **large plum tomatoes, cut into ½-inch chunks (2 cups)**
- 1 **cup fresh or thawed frozen corn kernels**
- ½ **to 1 teaspoon crushed dried rosemary**
- ¼ **cup grated Asiago or Parmesan cheese**
- 1 **tablespoon chopped fresh parsley**

Tip
Layer the ingredients in the order given to ensure they are all cooked properly.

Combine all ingredients except cheese and parsley in **CROCK-POT®** slow cooker; mix well. Cover. Cook on LOW 8 hours or on HIGH 5 hours or until vegetables are tender. Stir; ladle into shallow bowls. Top with cheese and parsley.

Makes 4 servings

Nutrition Information: Serving Size 1¼ cups, Calories 168, Total Fat 3g, Saturated Fat 7g, Protein 9g, Carbohydrate 28g, Cholesterol 3mg, Dietary Fiber 6g, Sodium 317mg

Mediterranean Stew

- **2** pounds butternut squash, peeled and cut into 1-inch cubes
- **2** cups unpeeled eggplant, cut into 1-inch cubes
- **2** cups sliced zucchini
- **1** can (15½ ounces) chickpeas, rinsed and drained
- **1** package (10 ounces) frozen cut okra
- **1** can (8 ounces) tomato sauce
- **1** cup chopped yellow onion
- **1** medium tomato, chopped
- **1** medium carrot, sliced
- **½** cup vegetable broth
- **⅓** cup raisins
- **1** clove garlic, minced
- **½** teaspoon ground cumin
- **½** teaspoon ground turmeric
- **¼** teaspoon ground red pepper
- **¼** teaspoon ground cinnamon
- **¼** teaspoon paprika
- **6** cups hot cooked couscous or rice (optional)

1. Combine all ingredients except couscous in **CROCK-POT®** slow cooker; mix well.

2. Cover; cook on LOW 8 to 10 hours or until vegetables are crisp-tender. Serve over couscous, garnished with parsley, if desired.

Makes 6 servings

Nutrition Information: Serving Size about 1¾ cups, Calories 389, Total Fat 2g, Saturated Fat 0g, Protein 13g, Carbohydrate 84g, Cholesterol 0mg, Dietary Fiber 12g, Sodium 470mg

Side Dishes

Braised Sweet and Sour Cabbage and Apples

- **2 tablespoons unsalted butter**
- **6 cups coarsely shredded red cabbage**
- **1 large sweet apple, peeled, cored and cut into bite-size pieces**
- **3 whole cloves**
- **½ cup raisins**
- **½ cup apple cider**
- **3 tablespoons cider vinegar, divided**
- **2 tablespoons packed dark brown sugar**
- **½ teaspoon salt**
- **¼ teaspoon black pepper**

1. Melt butter in very large skillet or shallow pot over medium heat. Add cabbage. Cook and stir 3 minutes until cabbage is glossy. Transfer to **CROCK-POT®** slow cooker.

2. Add apple, cloves, raisins, apple cider, 2 tablespoons vinegar, brown sugar, salt and pepper. Cover; cook on LOW 2½ to 3 hours.

3. To serve, remove cloves and stir in remaining 1 tablespoon vinegar.

Makes 6 servings

Nutrition Information: Serving Size about 1¼ cups, Calories 153, Total Fat 4g, Saturated Fat 2g, Protein 2g, Carbohydrate 29g, Cholesterol 10mg, Dietary Fiber 3g, Sodium 227mg

Side Dishes

Wild Rice with Fruit & Nuts

  2 **cups wild rice, rinsed***

  ½ **cup dried cranberries**

  ½ **cup chopped raisins**

  ½ **cup chopped dried apricots**

  ½ **cup slivered almonds, toasted****

  5 **cups 99% fat-free, reduced-sodium chicken broth**

  1 **cup orange juice**

  2 **tablespoons unsalted butter, melted**

  1 **teaspoon ground cumin**

  2 **green onions, thinly sliced**

  2 **tablespoons chopped fresh parsley**

     Salt and black pepper, to taste

*Do not use parboiled rice or a blend containing parboiled rice.

**To toast almonds, spread in single layer in heavy-bottomed skillet. Cook over medium heat 1 to 2 minutes, stirring frequently, until nuts are lightly browned. Remove from skillet immediately. Cool before using.

1. Combine wild rice, cranberries, raisins, apricots and almonds in **CROCK-POT**® slow cooker.

2. Combine broth, orange juice, butter and cumin in medium bowl. Pour mixture over rice and stir to mix.

3. Cover; cook on LOW 7 hours or on HIGH 2½ to 3 hours. Stir once, adding more hot broth if necessary.

4. When rice is soft, add green onions and parsley. Adjust seasonings, if desired. Cook 10 minutes longer and serve.

Makes 8 servings

Nutrition Information: Serving Size about ¾ cup, Calories 301, Total Fat 7g, Saturated Fat 2g, Protein 8g, Carbohydrate 54g, Cholesterol 8mg, Dietary Fiber 4g, Sodium 586mg

Skinny Corn Bread

- 1¼ cups all-purpose flour
- ¾ cup yellow cornmeal
- ¼ cup sugar
- 1 teaspoon baking powder
- 1 teaspoon baking soda
- ¼ teaspoon seasoned salt
- 1 cup fat-free buttermilk
- ¼ cup cholesterol-free egg substitute
- ¼ cup canola oil

Tip
This recipe works best in round **CROCK-POT®** slow cookers.

1. Coat 3-quart **CROCK-POT®** slow cooker with nonstick cooking spray.

2. Sift together flour, cornmeal, sugar, baking powder, baking soda and seasoned salt in large bowl. Make well in center of dry mixture. Pour in buttermilk, egg substitute and oil. Mix in dry ingredients just until moistened. Pour mixture into **CROCK-POT®** slow cooker.

3. Cook, covered, with lid slightly ajar to allow excess moisture to escape, on LOW 3 to 4 hours or on HIGH 45 minutes to 1½ hours, or until edges are golden and knife inserted into center comes out clean. Remove stoneware from **CROCK-POT®** slow cooker. Cool on wire rack about 10 minutes; remove bread from stoneware and cool completely on rack.

Makes 8 servings

Nutrition Information: Serving Size 1 slice (⅛ loaf), Calories 228, Total Fat 8g, Saturated Fat 1g, Protein 5g, Carbohydrate 35g, Cholesterol 1mg, Dietary Fiber 1g, Sodium 300mg

Wild Rice and Dried Cherry Risotto

1 **cup lightly salted dry-roasted peanuts**

2 **tablespoons sesame oil, divided**

1 **cup chopped yellow onion**

6 **ounces uncooked wild rice**

1 **cup diced carrots**

1 **cup chopped green or red bell pepper**

½ **cup dried cherries**

⅛ **teaspoon red pepper flakes**

4 **cups hot water**

¼ **cup reduced-sodium soy sauce**

½ **teaspoon salt, or to taste**

1. Coat **CROCK-POT®** slow cooker with nonstick cooking spray. Heat large skillet over medium-high heat until hot. Add peanuts. Cook and stir 2 to 3 minutes or until peanuts begin to brown. Transfer peanuts to plate; set aside.

2. Heat 2 teaspoons oil in skillet until hot. Add onion. Cook and stir 6 minutes or until richly browned. Transfer to **CROCK-POT®** slow cooker.

3. Stir in wild rice, carrots, bell pepper, cherries, pepper flakes and water. Cover; cook on HIGH 3 hours.

4. Let stand 15 minutes, uncovered, until rice absorbs liquid. Stir in soy sauce, peanuts, remaining oil and salt.

Makes 10 servings

Nutrition Information: Serving Size about ¾ cup, Calories 202, Total Fat 9g, Saturated Fat 1g, Protein 7g, Carbohydrate 24g, Cholesterol 0mg, Dietary Fiber 3g, Sodium 282mg

Cuban Black Beans and Rice

3¾ cups **99% fat-free, reduced-sodium chicken broth**

1½ cups **uncooked brown rice**

1 **large yellow onion, chopped**

1 **jalapeño pepper, seeded and chopped***

3 **cloves garlic, minced**

2 **teaspoons ground cumin**

1 **teaspoon salt**

2 **cans (15 ounces each) fat-free, no-salt-added black beans, rinsed and drained**

1 **tablespoon fresh lime juice**

Sour cream (optional)

Chopped green onions (optional)

*Jalapeño peppers can sting and irritate the skin, so wear rubber gloves when handling peppers and do not touch your eyes.

1. Place chicken broth, rice, onion, jalapeño pepper, garlic, cumin and salt in **CROCK-POT®** slow cooker, mixing well. Cover and cook on LOW 7½ hours or until rice is tender.

2. Stir in beans and lime juice. Cover and cook 15 to 20 minutes more or until beans are heated through. Garnish with sour cream and green onions, if desired.

Makes 6 servings

Nutrition Information: Serving Size about 1 cup, Calories 300, Total Fat 2g, Saturated Fat 0g, Protein 12g, Carbohydrate 59g, Cholesterol 0mg, Dietary Fiber 9g, Sodium 303mg

Side Dishes

Southwestern Corn and Beans

- 1 **tablespoon olive oil**
- 1 **large onion, diced**
- 1 **jalapeño pepper, diced***
- 1 **clove garlic, minced**
- 2 **cans (15 ounces each) no-salt-added light red kidney beans, rinsed and drained**
- 1 **bag (16 ounces) frozen corn, thawed**
- 1 **can (14½ ounces) no-salt-added diced tomatoes, undrained**
- 1 **green bell pepper, cut into 1-inch pieces**
- 2 **teaspoons medium-hot chili powder**
- ½ **teaspoon salt**
- ½ **teaspoon ground cumin**
- ½ **teaspoon black pepper**
- **Sour cream or plain yogurt (optional)**
- **Sliced black olives (optional)**

Jalapeño peppers can sting and irritate the skin, so wear rubber gloves when handling peppers and do not touch your eyes. Wash hands after handling.

Tip

For a party, spoon this colorful vegetarian dish into hollowed-out bell peppers or bread bowls.

1. Heat oil in medium skillet over medium heat. Add onion, jalapeño pepper and garlic; cook 5 minutes. Combine onion mixture, beans, corn, tomatoes with juice, bell pepper, chili powder, salt, cumin and black pepper in **CROCK-POT®** slow cooker; mix well. Cover; cook on LOW 7 to 8 hours or on HIGH 2 to 3 hours.

2. Serve with sour cream and black olives, if desired.

Makes 6 servings

Nutrition Information: Serving Size about 1¼ cups, Calories 230, Total Fat 3g, Saturated Fat 1g, Protein 12g, Carbohydrate 40g, Cholesterol 0mg, Dietary Fiber 15g, Sodium 276mg

Coconut-Lime Sweet Potatoes with Walnuts

2½ **pounds sweet potatoes, peeled and cut into 1-inch pieces**

  8 **ounces shredded, peeled carrots**

 ¾ **cup reduced-fat shredded coconut, divided**

  1 **tablespoon unsalted butter, melted**

  3 **tablespoons sugar**

 ½ **teaspoon salt**

 ⅓ **cup walnuts, toasted and coarsely chopped, divided**

  2 **teaspoons grated lime peel**

1. Combine sweet potatoes, carrots, ½ cup coconut, butter, sugar and salt in **CROCK-POT**® slow cooker. Cover and cook on LOW 5 to 6 hours, until sweet potatoes are tender and cooked through.

2. Meanwhile, add remaining ¼ cup coconut in preheated small nonstick skillet. Cook, shaking pan often, until coconut is lightly browned, about 4 minutes. Transfer to a small bowl and cool completely.

3. Mash sweet potatoes. Stir in 3 tablespoons walnuts and lime peel. Sprinkle top of mashed sweet potatoes with remaining walnuts and toasted coconut. Serve warm.

Makes 8 servings

Nutrition Information: Serving Size about ¾ cup, Calories 207, Total Fat 6g, Saturated Fat 2g, Protein 3g, Carbohydrate 37g, Cholesterol 4mg, Dietary Fiber 6g, Sodium 243mg

Lemon Dilled Parsnips and Turnips

  2 cups 99% fat-free chicken broth

  ¼ cup chopped green onions

  4 tablespoons lemon juice

  4 tablespoons dried dill

  1 teaspoon minced garlic

  4 turnips, peeled and cut into ½-inch pieces

  3 parsnips, peeled and cut into ½-inch pieces

  4 tablespoons cornstarch

  ¼ cup cold water

1. Combine broth, onions, lemon juice, dill and garlic in **CROCK-POT®** slow cooker.

2. Add turnips and parsnips; stir. Cover; cook on LOW 3 to 4 hours or on HIGH 1 to 3 hours.

3. Turn **CROCK-POT®** slow cooker to HIGH. Dissolve cornstarch in water. Add to **CROCK-POT®** slow cooker. Stir well to combine. Cover; continue cooking 15 minutes longer or until thickened.

Makes 10 servings

Nutrition Information: Serving Size about ¾ cup, Calories 70, Total Fat 0g, Saturated Fat 0g, Protein 2g, Carbohydrate 16g, Cholesterol 0mg, Dietary Fiber 3g, Sodium 226mg

Jim's Mexican-Style Spinach

3 packages (10 ounces each) frozen chopped spinach

1 tablespoon canola oil

1 onion, chopped

1 clove garlic, minced

2 Anaheim chiles, roasted, peeled and minced*

3 fresh tomatillos, roasted, husks removed and chopped**

6 tablespoons fat-free sour cream (optional)

To roast chiles, heat heavy frying pan over medium-high heat until drop of water sizzles. Cook chiles, turning occasionally with tongs, until blackened all over. (Or hold directly over gas flame with long-handled fork.) Place chiles in brown paper bag for 2 to 5 minutes. Remove chiles from bag and scrape off charred skin. Cut off top with seed core. Cut lengthwise into halves and with a knife tip, scrape out veins and any remaining seeds.

**To roast fresh tomatillos, heat heavy frying pan over medium heat. Leaving papery husks on, roast tomatillos, turning often, until husks are brown and interior flesh is soft, about 10 minutes. When cool enough to handle, remove and discard husks.*

1. Place frozen spinach in **CROCK-POT®** slow cooker.

2. Heat oil in large skillet over medium heat until hot. Cook and stir onion and garlic until onion is soft but not browned, about 5 minutes. Add chiles and tomatillos; cook 3 to 4 minutes longer. Add mixture to **CROCK-POT®** slow cooker.

3. Cover; cook on LOW 4 to 6 hours. Stir before serving. Serve with dollops of sour cream, if desired.

Makes 6 servings

Nutrition Information: Serving Size about ¾ cup, Calories 81, Total Fat 3g, Saturated Fat 0g, Protein 6g, Carbohydrate 10g, Cholesterol 0mg, Dietary Fiber 5g, Sodium 107mg

Side Dishes

Easy Dirty Rice

- ½ **pound reduced-fat Italian sausage**
- 2 **cups water**
- 1 **cup uncooked long-grain rice**
- 1 **large yellow onion, finely chopped**
- 1 **large green bell pepper, finely chopped**
- ½ **cup finely chopped celery**
- ¼ **teaspoon salt**
- ½ **teaspoon ground red pepper**
- ½ **cup chopped fresh parsley**

Tip
Try substituting brown rice for the white rice in this recipe. Since it contains the bran and the germ, it is more nutritious than ordinary white rice.

1. Brown sausage in skillet 6 to 8 minutes over medium-high heat, stirring to break up meat. Transfer to **CROCK-POT®** slow cooker, discarding any drippings from skillet.

2. Stir in remaining ingredients except parsley. Cover; cook on LOW 2 hours. Stir in parsley.

Makes 4 servings

Nutrition Information: Serving Size about ¾ cup, Calories 192, Total Fat 5g, Saturated Fat 2g, Protein 7g, Carbohydrate 29g, Cholesterol 18mg, Dietary Fiber 2g, Sodium 273mg

Side Dishes

Parmesan Potato Wedges

    2 **pounds red potatoes, cut into ½-inch wedges**
  ¼ **cup finely chopped yellow onion**
1½ **teaspoons dried oregano**
  ½ **teaspoon salt**
  ¼ **teaspoon black pepper, or to taste**
    2 **tablespoons butter, cut into ⅛-inch pieces**
  ¼ **cup (1 ounce) grated Parmesan cheese**

Layer potatoes, onion, oregano, salt, pepper and butter in **CROCK-POT®** slow cooker. Cover; cook on HIGH 4 hours. Transfer potatoes to serving platter and sprinkle with cheese.

Makes 6 servings

Nutrition Information: Serving Size about ¾ cup, Calories 160, Total Fat 5g, Saturated Fat 3g, Protein 5g, Carbohydrate 25g, Cholesterol 14mg, Dietary Fiber 3g, Sodium 269mg

Lentils with Walnuts

    1 **cup brown lentils**
    1 **small yellow onion, chopped**
    1 **stalk celery, trimmed and chopped**
    1 **large carrot, chopped**
  ¼ **teaspoon crushed dried thyme**
    3 **cups fat-free, reduced-sodium chicken broth**
       Salt and black pepper, to taste
  ¼ **cup chopped walnuts**

1. Combine lentils, onion, celery, carrot, thyme and broth in **CROCK-POT®** slow cooker. Cover; cook on HIGH 3 hours. Do not overcook. (Lentils should absorb most or all of broth. Slightly tilt **CROCK-POT®** slow cooker to check.)

2. Season with salt and pepper. Spoon lentils into serving bowl and sprinkle on walnuts.

Makes 6 servings

Nutrition Information: Serving Size ¾ cup, Calories 158, Total Fat 4g, Saturated Fat 0g, Protein 10g, Carbohydrate 22g, Cholesterol 0mg, Dietary Fiber 10g, Sodium 241mg

Parmesan Potato Wedges

Orange-Spice Glazed Carrots

1 **package (32 ounces) baby carrots**

½ **cup packed light brown sugar**

½ **cup orange juice**

1 **tablespoon unsalted butter**

¾ **teaspoon ground cinnamon**

¼ **teaspoon ground nutmeg**

¼ **cup cold water**

2 **tablespoons cornstarch**

1. Combine carrots, sugar, orange juice, butter, cinnamon and nutmeg in **CROCK-POT®** slow cooker. Cover; cook on LOW 3½ to 4 hours or until carrots are crisp-tender.

2. Spoon carrots into serving bowl. Transfer cooking liquid to small saucepan. Bring to a boil.

3. Mix water and cornstarch until smooth; stir into saucepan. Boil 1 minute or until thickened, stirring constantly. Spoon over carrots.

Makes 6 servings

Nutrition Information: Serving Size about ¾ cup, Calories 179, Total Fat 2g, Saturated Fat 1g, Protein 2g, Carbohydrate 39g, Cholesterol 5mg, Dietary Fiber 4g, Sodium 6mg

Herbed Fall Vegetables

  2 medium Yukon Gold potatoes, peeled and cut into ½-inch dice

  2 medium sweet potatoes, peeled and cut into ½-inch dice

  3 parsnips, peeled and cut into ½-inch dice

  1 medium head of fennel, sliced and cut into ½-inch dice

  ¾ cup chopped fresh herbs, such as tarragon, parsley, sage or thyme

  2 tablespoons unsalted butter, cut into small pieces

  1 cup fat-free, reduced-sodium chicken broth

  1 tablespoon salt

     Freshly ground black pepper, to taste

1. Combine potatoes, parsnips, fennel, herbs and butter in **CROCK-POT**® slow cooker.

2. Whisk together broth, salt and pepper in small bowl. Pour mixture over vegetables. Cover; cook on LOW 4½ hours or on HIGH 3 hours or until vegetables are tender, stirring occasionally to ensure even cooking.

Makes 6 servings

Nutrition Information: Serving Size about 1 cup, Calories 135, Total Fat 3g, Saturated Fat 2g, Protein 3g, Carbohydrate 26g, Cholesterol 8mg, Dietary Fiber 6g, Sodium 244mg

Winter Squash and Apples

- ¾ **teaspoon salt**
- ½ **teaspoon black pepper**
- 1 **butternut squash (about 2 pounds), peeled and seeded**
- 2 **apples, cored and cut into slices**
- 1 **medium yellow onion, quartered and sliced**
- 1½ **tablespoons unsalted butter**

1. Combine salt and pepper in small bowl; set aside.

2. Cut squash into 2-inch pieces; place in **CROCK-POT**® slow cooker. Add apples and onion. Sprinkle with salt mixture; stir well. Cover; cook on LOW 6 to 7 hours or until vegetables are tender.

3. Just before serving, stir in butter and season to taste with additional salt and pepper.

Makes 6 servings

Nutrition Information: Serving Size about ¾ cup, Calories 133, Total Fat 3g, Saturated Fat 2g, Protein 2g, Carbohydrate 28g, Cholesterol 8mg, Dietary Fiber 5g, Sodium 299mg

Barley with Currants and Pine Nuts

½ **tablespoon unsalted butter**

1 **small onion, finely chopped**

½ **cup pearl barley**

2 **cups fat-free, reduced-sodium chicken broth**

½ **teaspoon salt, or to taste**

¼ **teaspoon black pepper**

⅓ **cup currants**

¼ **cup pine nuts**

1. Melt butter in small skillet over medium-high heat. Add onion. Cook and stir until lightly browned, about 2 minutes. Transfer to **CROCK-POT®** slow cooker. Add barley, broth, salt and pepper. Stir in currants. Cover; cook on LOW 3 hours.

2. Stir in pine nuts and serve immediately.

Makes 4 servings

Nutrition Information: Serving Size about ½ cup, Calories 197, Total Fat 8g, Saturated Fat 1g, Protein 5g, Carbohydrate 30g, Cholesterol 4mg, Dietary Fiber 5g, Sodium 228mg

Orange-Spiced Sweet Potatoes

- **2 pounds sweet potatoes, peeled and diced**
- **½ cup packed dark brown sugar**
- **2 tablespoons unsalted butter, cut into small pieces**
- **1 teaspoon ground cinnamon**
- **½ teaspoon ground nutmeg**
- **½ teaspoon grated orange peel**
  Juice of 1 medium orange
- **¼ teaspoon salt**
- **1 teaspoon vanilla**
  Chopped toasted pecans (optional)

Tip

For a creamy variation, mash potatoes with a hand masher or electric mixer, and add ¼ cup milk or whipping cream for moist consistency. Sprinkle with cinnamon-sugar, and sprinkle on toasted pecans, if desired.

Place all ingredients except pecans in **CROCK-POT®** slow cooker. Cover; cook on LOW 4 hours or on HIGH 2 hours or until potatoes are tender. Sprinkle with pecans before serving, if desired.

Makes 8 servings

Nutrition Information: Serving Size about ¾ cup, Calories 198, Total Fat 5g, Saturated Fat 2g, Protein 2g, Carbohydrate 38g, Cholesterol 8mg, Dietary Fiber 4g, Sodium 140mg

Red Cabbage and Apples

  1 **small head red cabbage, cored and thinly sliced**

  1 **large apple, peeled and grated**

 ¾ **cup sugar**

 ½ **cup red wine vinegar**

  1 **teaspoon ground cloves**

 ½ **cup crisp-cooked and crumbled bacon (optional)**

     Fresh apple slices (optional)

Combine cabbage, grated apples, sugar, vinegar and cloves in **CROCK-POT**® slow cooker. Cover; cook on HIGH 6 hours, stirring after 3 hours. To serve, sprinkle with bacon and garnish with apple slices, if desired.

Makes 6 servings

Nutrition Information: Serving Size about ¾ cup, Calories 147, Total Fat 0g, Saturated Fat 0g, Protein 1g, Carbohydrate 37g, Cholesterol 0mg, Dietary Fiber 3g, Sodium 29mg

Garlic and Herb Polenta

- 8 **cups water**
- 2 **cups yellow cornmeal**
- 2 **teaspoons finely minced garlic**
- 2 **teaspoons salt**
- 1 **tablespoon unsalted butter, divided**
- 3 **tablespoons chopped fresh herbs such as parsley, chives, thyme or chervil (or a combination of any of these)**

Tip

Polenta may also be poured into a greased pan and allowed to cool until set. Cut into squares (or slice as desired) to serve. For even more great flavor, chill polenta slices until firm then grill or fry until golden brown.

Coat **CROCK-POT®** slow cooker with nonstick cooking spray. Add water, cornmeal, garlic, salt and butter; stir. Cover and cook on LOW 4 hours or on HIGH 3 hours, stirring occasionally. Stir in chopped herbs just before serving.

Makes 6 servings

Nutrition Information: Serving Size about ⅔ cup, Calories 168, Total Fat 2g, Saturated Fat 1g, Protein 3g, Carbohydrate 32g, Cholesterol 4mg, Dietary Fiber 2g, Sodium 303mg

Rustic Cheddar Mashed Potatoes

- **2 pounds russet potatoes, peeled and diced**
- **1 cup water**
- **2 tablespoons unsalted butter, cut into small pieces**
- **¾ cup nonfat milk**
- **¾ teaspoon salt**
- **½ teaspoon black pepper**
- **½ cup finely chopped green onions**
- **2 tablespoons reduced-fat shredded Cheddar cheese**

1. Combine potatoes and water in **CROCK-POT®** slow cooker; dot with butter. Cover; cook on LOW 6 hours or on HIGH 3 hours, or until potatoes are tender. Transfer potatoes to large mixing bowl.

2. Using electric mixer at medium speed, whip potatoes until well blended. Add milk, salt and pepper; whip until well blended.

3. Stir in green onions and cheese; cover. Let stand 15 minutes to allow flavors to blend and cheese to melt.

Makes 8 servings

Nutrition Information: Serving Size about ¾ cup, Calories 127, Total Fat 3g, Saturated Fat 2g, Protein 3g, Carbohydrate 22g, Cholesterol 10mg, Dietary Fiber 2g, Sodium 246mg

Spinach Gorgonzola Corn Bread

- **2 boxes (8½ ounces each) corn bread mix**
- **3 eggs**
- **½ cup fat-free half-and-half**
- **1 box (10 ounces) frozen chopped spinach, thawed and drained**
- **½ cup crumbled Gorgonzola**
- **1 teaspoon black pepper**
- **Paprika (optional)**

Note
Cook only on **HIGH** setting for proper crust and texture.

1. Coat 4½-quart **CROCK-POT**® slow cooker with nonstick cooking spray.

2. Mix all ingredients in medium bowl. Place batter in **CROCK-POT**® slow cooker. Cover; cook on HIGH 1½ hours. Sprinkle top with paprika for more colorful crust, if desired. Let bread cool completely before inverting onto serving platter.

Makes 12 servings

Nutrition Information: Serving Size 1 slice (⅟₁₂ loaf), Calories 134, Total Fat 4g, Saturated Fat 2g, Protein 9g, Carbohydrate 15g, Cholesterol 61mg, Dietary Fiber 3g, Sodium 251mg

Risi Bisi

- 1½ **cups uncooked converted long-grain rice**
- ¾ **cup chopped yellow onion**
- 2 **cloves garlic, minced**
- 2 **cans (about 14 ounces each) reduced-sodium chicken broth**
- ⅓ **cup water**
- ¾ **teaspoon Italian seasoning**
- ½ **teaspoon dried basil**
- ½ **cup frozen peas**
- ¼ **cup grated Parmesan cheese**
- ¼ **cup toasted pine nuts (optional)**

1. Combine rice, onion and garlic in **CROCK-POT®** slow cooker.

2. Bring broth and water to a boil in small saucepan. Stir broth mixture, Italian seasoning and basil into rice mixture in **CROCK-POT®** slow cooker. Cover; cook on LOW 2 to 3 hours or until liquid is absorbed.

3. Add peas. Cover; cook on LOW 1 hour. Stir in cheese. Sprinkle with pine nuts, if desired.

Makes 6 servings

Nutrition Information: Serving Size about ½ cup, Calories 158, Total Fat 1g, Saturated Fat 1g, Protein 5g, Carbohydrate 31g, Cholesterol 2mg, Dietary Fiber 1g, Sodium 279mg

Side Dishes

Pesto Rice and Beans

1 can (15 ounces) no-salt-added Great Northern beans, rinsed and drained

1 can (14 ounces) fat-free, reduced-sodium chicken broth

¾ cup uncooked converted long-grain rice

1½ cups frozen cut green beans, thawed and drained

½ cup prepared pesto

Grated Parmesan cheese (optional)

Tip

Choose converted long-grain rice (or Arborio rice when suggested) or wild rice for best results. Long, slow cooking can turn other types of rice into mush; if you prefer to use another type of rice instead of converted rice, cook it on the stove-top and add it to the **CROCK-POT**® slow cooker during the last 15 minutes of cooking.

1. Combine beans, broth and rice in **CROCK-POT**® slow cooker. Cover; cook on LOW 2 hours.

2. Stir in green beans. Cover; cook 1 hour or until rice and beans are tender.

3. Turn off **CROCK-POT**® slow cooker and transfer stoneware to heatproof surface. Stir in pesto and Parmesan cheese, if desired. Let stand, covered, 5 minutes or until cheese is melted. Serve immediately.

Makes 8 servings

Nutrition Information: Serving Size ½ cup, Calories 195, Total Fat 8g, Saturated Fat 2g, Protein 7g, Carbohydrate 24g, Cholesterol 5mg, Dietary Fiber 5g, Sodium 245mg

Greek Rice

2	tablespoons unsalted butter
1¾	cups uncooked converted long-grain rice
2	cans (14 ounces each) fat-free, reduced-sodium chicken broth
1	teaspoon Greek seasoning
1	teaspoon ground oregano
1	cup pitted kalamata olives, drained and chopped
¾	cup chopped roasted red peppers
	Crumbled feta cheese (optional)
	Chopped fresh Italian parsley (optional)

Melt butter in large nonstick skillet over medium-high heat. Add rice and sauté 4 minutes or until golden brown. Transfer to **CROCK-POT®** slow cooker. Stir in chicken broth, Greek seasoning and oregano. Cover and cook on LOW 4 hours or until liquid has all been absorbed and rice is tender. Stir in olives and roasted red peppers and cook 5 minutes more. Garnish with feta and Italian parsley, if desired.

Makes 8 servings

Nutrition Information: Serving Size ¾ cup, Calories 175, Total Fat 4g, Saturated Fat 2g, Protein 3g, Carbohydrate 32g, Cholesterol 8mg, Dietary Fiber 0g, Sodium 297mg

Spiced Sweet Potatoes

2 pounds sweet potatoes, peeled and cut into ½-inch pieces

¼ cup packed dark brown sugar

1 teaspoon ground cinnamon

½ teaspoon ground nutmeg

⅛ teaspoon salt

2 tablespoons unsalted butter, cut into small pieces

1 teaspoon vanilla

1. Combine potatoes, brown sugar, cinnamon, nutmeg and salt in **CROCK-POT®** slow cooker; mix well. Cover; cook on LOW 7 hours or on HIGH 4 hours.

2. Add butter and vanilla; gently stir to blend.

Makes 4 servings

Nutrition Information: Serving Size about 1 cup, Calories 258, Total Fat 3g, Saturated Fat 2g, Protein 4g, Carbohydrate 8g, Cholesterol 8mg, Dietary Fiber 7g, Sodium 196mg

Green Bean Casserole

2 **packages (10 ounces each) frozen green beans, thawed**

1 **can (10¾ ounces) low-sodium condensed cream of mushroom soup, undiluted**

1 **tablespoon chopped parsley**

1 **tablespoon chopped roasted red peppers**

1 **teaspoon dried sage**

½ **teaspoon salt**

½ **teaspoon black pepper**

¼ **teaspoon ground nutmeg**

½ **cup toasted slivered almonds**

Combine all ingredients except almonds in **CROCK-POT**® slow cooker. Cover; cook on LOW 3 to 4 hours. Sprinkle with almonds before serving.

Makes 6 servings

Nutrition Information: Serving Size about ¾ cup, Calories 91, Total Fat 7g, Saturated Fat 1g, Protein 4g, Carbohydrate 13g, Cholesterol 2mg, Dietary Fiber 4g, Sodium 221mg

Desserts

Five-Spice Apple Crisp

- **1 tablespoon unsalted butter, melted**
- **6 Golden Delicious apples, peeled, cored and cut into ½-inch-thick slices**
- **2 teaspoons fresh lemon juice**
- **¼ cup packed light brown sugar**
- **¾ teaspoon Chinese five-spice powder or ½ teaspoon ground cinnamon and ¼ teaspoon ground allspice**
- **1 cup coarsely crushed almond biscotti**
- **Sweetened whipped cream (optional)**

1. Brush 4½-quart **CROCK-POT®** slow cooker with melted butter. Add apples and lemon juice and toss to combine. Sprinkle with brown sugar and five-spice powder and toss again.

2. Cover; cook for 3½ hours on LOW or until apples are tender. Sprinkle cookies over apples. Spoon into bowls and serve warm, garnished with whipped cream, if desired.

Makes 6 servings

Nutrition Information: Serving Size ⅙ crisp, Calories 211, Total Fat 4g, Saturated Fat 2g, Protein 2g, Carbohydrate 44g, Cholesterol 5mg, Dietary Fiber 4g, Sodium 50mg

Desserts

English Bread Pudding

- **16 slices day-old, firm-textured white bread (1 small loaf)**
- **1¾ cups nonfat milk**
- **1 package (8 ounces) mixed dried fruit, cut into small pieces**
- **¼ cup chopped walnuts**
- **1 medium apple, seeded and chopped**
- **⅓ cup packed brown sugar**
- **2 tablespoons unsalted butter, melted**
- **1 egg, lightly beaten**
- **1 teaspoon ground cinnamon**
- **¼ teaspoon ground nutmeg**
- **¼ teaspoon ground cloves**

Note

Chopping dried fruits can be difficult. To make the job easier, cut fruit with kitchen scissors. Spray scissors (or your chef's knife) with nonstick cooking spray before chopping, to prevent sticking.

1. Tear bread, with crusts, into 1- to 2-inch pieces; place in **CROCK-POT®** slow cooker. Pour milk over bread; let soak 30 minutes. Stir in dried fruit, nuts and apple.

2. Combine remaining ingredients in small bowl; pour over bread mixture. Stir well to blend. Cover; cook on LOW 3½ to 4 hours or until skewer inserted into center of pudding comes out clean.

Makes 8 servings

Nutrition Information: Serving Size about 1 cup, Calories 264, Total Fat 7g, Saturated Fat 2g, Protein 6g, Carbohydrate 49g, Cholesterol 28mg, Dietary Fiber 3g, Sodium 245mg

 **Desserts**

Poached Autumn Fruits with Vanilla-Citrus Broth

2 **Granny Smith apples, peeled, cored and halved (reserve cores)**

2 **Bartlett pears, peeled, cored and halved (reserve cores)**

1 **orange, peeled and halved**

5 **tablespoons honey**

1 **vanilla bean, split and seeded (reserve seeds)**

1 **cinnamon stick**

⅓ **cup sugar**

Vanilla ice cream (optional)

1. Place apple and pear cores in **CROCK-POT®** slow cooker. Squeeze juice from orange halves into **CROCK-POT®** slow cooker. Add orange halves, honey, vanilla bean and seeds, cinnamon and sugar. Add apples and pears. Pour in enough water to cover fruit. Stir gently to combine. Cover; cook on HIGH 2 hours or until fruit is tender.

2. Remove apple and pear halves; set aside. Strain cooking liquid into large saucepan. (Discard solids.) Simmer gently over low heat until liquid reduces by half and thickens.

3. Dice apple and pear halves. Add to saucepan to rewarm fruit. To serve, spoon fruit with sauce into bowls. Top with vanilla ice cream, if desired.

Makes 6 servings

Nutrition Information: Serving Size about ¾ cup fruit and broth, Calories 175, Total Fat 0g, Saturated Fat 0g, Protein 1g, Carbohydrate 46g, Cholesterol 0mg, Dietary Fiber 4g, Sodium 2mg

Mixed Berry Cobbler

    1 **package (16 ounces)
       frozen mixed berries**

    ¾ **cup granulated sugar**

    2 **tablespoons quick-cooking tapioca**

    2 **teaspoons grated lemon peel**

  1½ **cups all-purpose flour**

    ½ **cup packed light brown sugar**

  2¼ **teaspoons baking powder**

    ¼ **teaspoon ground nutmeg**

    ¾ **cup 2% milk**

    2 **tablespoons unsalted butter, melted**

       **Vanilla ice cream or whipped cream
       (optional)**

Tip

Cobblers are year-round favorites. Experiment with seasonal fresh fruits, such as pears, plums, peaches, rhubarb, blueberries, raspberries, strawberries, blackberries or gooseberries. Or try different apple varieties, including newer ones such as Pink Lady, or a blend of your favorite apples to come up with your own signature cobbler.

1. Coat **CROCK-POT**® slow cooker with nonstick cooking spray. Stir together berries, granulated sugar, tapioca and lemon peel in medium bowl. Transfer to **CROCK-POT**® slow cooker.

2. For topping, combine flour, brown sugar, baking powder and nutmeg in medium bowl. Add milk and butter; stir just until blended. Drop spoonfuls of dough on top of berry mixture. Cover; cook on LOW 4 hours. Uncover; let stand about 30 minutes. Serve with ice cream, if desired.

Makes 8 servings

Nutrition Information: Serving Size ⅛ cobbler, Calories 228, Total Fat 3g, Saturated Fat 2g, Protein 3g, Carbohydrate 49g, Cholesterol 8mg, Dietary Fiber 2g, Sodium 111mg

Desserts

Fresh Berry Compote

- **2 cups fresh blueberries**
- **4 cups fresh sliced strawberries**
- **2 tablespoons orange juice**
- **½ cup sugar**
- **4 slices (½ × 1½ inches) lemon peel with no white pith**
- **1 cinnamon stick or ½ teaspoon ground cinnamon**

Tip

To turn this compote into a fresh-fruit topping for cake, ice cream, waffles or pancakes, carefully spoon out fruit, leaving cooking liquid in **CROCK-POT®** slow cooker. Blend 1 to 2 tablespoons cornstarch with ¼ cup cold water until smooth. Add to cooking liquid and cook on HIGH until thickened. Return fruit to sauce and blend in gently.

1. Place blueberries in **CROCK-POT®** slow cooker. Cover; cook on HIGH 45 minutes until blueberries begin to soften.

2. Add strawberries, orange juice, ½ cup sugar, lemon peel and cinnamon stick. Stir to blend. Cover; cook on HIGH 1 to 1½ hours or until berries soften and sugar dissolves. Check for sweetness and add more sugar if necessary, cooking until added sugar dissolves.

3. Remove insert from **CROCK-POT®** slow cooker to heatproof surface and let cool. Serve compote warm or chilled.

Makes 4 servings

Nutrition Information: Serving Size about 1½ cups fruit and sauce, Calories 214, Total Fat 1g, Saturated Fat 0g, Protein 2g, Carbohydrate 55g, Cholesterol 0mg, Dietary Fiber 7g, Sodium 4mg

Classic Baked Apples

¼ **cup packed dark brown sugar**

2 **tablespoons golden raisins**

1 **teaspoon grated lemon peel**

6 **medium baking apples, washed and cored**

1 **teaspoon ground cinnamon**

2 **tablespoons unsalted butter, cut into small pieces**

¼ **cup orange juice**

¼ **cup water**

Whipped cream (optional)

1. Combine brown sugar, raisins and lemon peel in small bowl. Fill core of each apple with mixture. Place apples in **CROCK-POT®** slow cooker. Sprinkle with cinnamon and dot with butter. Pour orange juice and water over apples. Cover; cook on LOW 7 to 9 hours or on HIGH 2½ to 3½ hours.

2. To serve, place apples in individual bowls. Top with sauce. Garnish with whipped cream, if desired.

Makes 6 servings

Nutrition Information: Serving Size 1 apple, Calories 180, Total Fat 4g, Saturated Fat 2g, Protein 1g, Carbohydrate 38g, Cholesterol 10mg, Dietary Fiber 5g, Sodium 6mg

Desserts

Peach Cobbler

- **2 packages (16 ounces each) frozen peaches, thawed and drained**
- **¾ cup plus 1 tablespoon sugar, divided**
- **2 teaspoons ground cinnamon, divided**
- **½ teaspoon ground nutmeg**
- **¾ cup all-purpose flour**
- **2 tablespoons unsalted butter, melted**
- **Whipped cream (optional)**

Tip

To make cleanup easier when cooking sticky or sugary foods, spray the inside of the **CROCK-POT®** slow cooker with nonstick cooking spray before adding ingredients.

1. Combine peaches, ¾ cup sugar, 1½ teaspoons cinnamon and nutmeg in medium bowl. Transfer to **CROCK-POT®** slow cooker.

2. For topping, combine flour, remaining 1 tablespoon sugar and remaining ½ teaspoon cinnamon in small bowl. Drizzle with melted butter and toss to coat. Sprinkle over peach mixture. Cover; cook on HIGH 2 hours. Serve with freshly whipped cream, if desired.

Makes 6 servings

Nutrition Information: Serving Size ⅙ cobbler, Calories 189, Total Fat 3g, Saturated Fat 7g, Protein 2g, Carbohydrate 41g, Cholesterol 8mg, Dietary Fiber 2g, Sodium 1mg

Poached Pears with Raspberry Sauce

- **4 cups cranberry-apple-raspberry juice cocktail**
- **2 cups Riesling wine**
- **¼ cup sugar**
- **2 cinnamon sticks, broken into halves**
- **5 firm Bosc or Anjou pears, peeled**
- **1 package (10 ounces) frozen raspberries in syrup, thawed**
- **Fresh berries (optional)**

1. Combine juice, wine, sugar and cinnamon stick halves in **CROCK-POT®** slow cooker. Submerge pears in mixture. Cover; cook on LOW 3½ to 4 hours or until pears are tender.

2. Remove and discard cinnamon sticks.

3. Process raspberries in food processor or blender until smooth; strain and discard seeds. Spoon raspberry sauce onto serving plates; place pears on top of sauce. Garnish with fresh berries, if desired.

Makes 5 servings

Nutrition Information: Serving Size 1 pear and ¼ cup sauce, Calories 390, Total Fat 0g, Saturated Fat 0g, Protein 1g, Carbohydrate 86g, Cholesterol 0mg, Dietary Fiber 7g, Sodium 35mg

Desserts

Apple-Date Crisp

6 cups thinly sliced, peeled apples (about 6 medium apples, preferably Golden Delicious)

2 teaspoons lemon juice

⅓ cup chopped dates

1⅓ cups uncooked quick oats

½ cup all-purpose flour

½ cup packed light brown sugar

½ teaspoon ground cinnamon

¼ teaspoon ground ginger

¼ teaspoon salt

Dash ground nutmeg

Dash ground cloves (optional)

2 tablespoons unsalted butter, melted

1. Coat **CROCK-POT®** slow cooker with nonstick cooking spray. Place apples in medium bowl. Sprinkle with lemon juice; toss to coat. Add dates and mix well. Transfer mixture to **CROCK-POT®** slow cooker.

2. For topping, combine oats, flour, sugar, cinnamon, ginger, salt, nutmeg and cloves, if desired, in medium bowl. Drizzle with melted butter and toss to coat. Sprinkle oat mixture over apples. Cover; cook on LOW about 4 hours or on HIGH about 2 hours, or until apples are tender.

Makes 6 servings

Nutrition Information: Serving Size ⅙ crisp, Calories 252, Total Fat 4g, Saturated Fat 2g, Protein 3g, Carbohydrate 53g, Cholesterol 8mg, Dietary Fiber 6g, Sodium 178mg

Cherry Rice Pudding

1½ **cups milk**

1 **cup hot cooked rice**

3 **eggs, beaten**

½ **cup sugar**

¼ **cup dried cherries or cranberries**

½ **teaspoon almond extract**

¼ **teaspoon salt**

Ground nutmeg (optional)

1. Combine all ingredients, except nutmeg, in large bowl. Pour into greased 1½-quart casserole dish. Cover dish with buttered aluminum foil, butter side down.

2. Place rack in **CROCK-POT**® slow cooker and pour in 1 cup water. Place casserole on rack. Cover; cook on LOW 4 to 5 hours.

3. Remove casserole from **CROCK-POT**® slow cooker. Let stand 15 minutes before serving. Garnish with nutmeg, if desired.

Makes 6 servings

Nutrition Information: Serving Size about ¾ cup, Calories 193, Total Fat 4g, Saturated Fat 1g, Protein 6g, Carbohydrate 33g, Cholesterol 111mg, Dietary Fiber 1g, Sodium 162mg

Desserts

Warm Spiced Apples and Pears

2 tablespoons unsalted butter

1 cup packed brown sugar

½ cup water

1 teaspoon vanilla extract

½ lemon, sliced

1 cinnamon stick, broken in half

½ teaspoon ground cloves

5 pears, quartered and cored

5 small Granny Smith apples, quartered and cored

Tip
Simmer a sweet treat in your **CROCK-POT®** slow cooker during dinner, so you can delight your family and guests with an appetizing warm dessert.

1. Melt butter in saucepan over medium heat. Add brown sugar, water, vanilla extract, lemon slices, cinnamon stick and cloves. Bring to a boil; cook and stir 1 minute. Remove from heat.

2. Combine pears, apples and butter mixture in **CROCK-POT®** slow cooker; mix well. Cover; cook on LOW 3½ to 4 hours or on HIGH 2 hours. Stir every 45 minutes to ensure even cooking.

Makes 8 servings

Nutrition Information: Serving Size about 1¼ cups fruit and sauce, Calories 246, Total Fat 3g, Saturated Fat 2g, Protein 1g, Carbohydrate 58g, Cholesterol 8mg, Dietary Fiber 6g, Sodium 11mg

Pumpkin-Cranberry Custard

- **1 can (30 ounces) pumpkin pie filling**
- **1 can (12 ounces) evaporated milk**
- **1 cup dried cranberries**
- **4 eggs, beaten**
- **1 cup crushed or whole gingersnap cookies (optional)**
- **Whipped cream (optional)**

Combine pumpkin, evaporated milk, cranberries and eggs in **CROCK-POT®** slow cooker; mix thoroughly. Cover; cook on HIGH 4 to 4½ hours. Serve with crushed or whole gingersnaps and whipped cream, if desired.

Makes 8 servings

Nutrition Information: Serving Size about ¾ cup, Calories 267, Total Fat 5g, Saturated Fat 3g, Protein 8g, Carbohydrate 60g, Cholesterol 16mg, Dietary Fiber 13g, Sodium 392mg

Index

Index

Index

Index

Index

Index

Index

Metric Chart

VOLUME MEASUREMENTS (dry)

1/8 teaspoon = 0.5 mL
1/4 teaspoon = 1 mL
1/2 teaspoon = 2 mL
3/4 teaspoon = 4 mL
1 teaspoon = 5 mL
1 tablespoon = 15 mL
2 tablespoons = 30 mL
1/4 cup = 60 mL
1/3 cup = 75 mL
1/2 cup = 125 mL
2/3 cup = 150 mL
3/4 cup = 175 mL
1 cup = 250 mL
2 cups = 1 pint = 500 mL
3 cups = 750 mL
4 cups = 1 quart = 1 L

VOLUME MEASUREMENTS (fluid)

1 fluid ounce (2 tablespoons) = 30 mL
4 fluid ounces (1/2 cup) = 125 mL
8 fluid ounces (1 cup) = 250 mL
12 fluid ounces (1 1/2 cups) = 375 mL
16 fluid ounces (2 cups) = 500 mL

WEIGHTS (mass)

1/2 ounce = 15 g
1 ounce = 30 g
3 ounces = 90 g
4 ounces = 120 g
8 ounces = 225 g
10 ounces = 285 g
12 ounces = 360 g
16 ounces = 1 pound = 450 g

DIMENSIONS

1/16 inch = 2 mm
1/8 inch = 3 mm
1/4 inch = 6 mm
1/2 inch = 1.5 cm
3/4 inch = 2 cm
1 inch = 2.5 cm

OVEN TEMPERATURES

250°F = 120°C
275°F = 140°C
300°F = 150°C
325°F = 160°C
350°F = 180°C
375°F = 190°C
400°F = 200°C
425°F = 220°C
450°F = 230°C

BAKING PAN AND DISH EQUIVALENTS

Utensil	Size in Inches	Size in Centimeters	Volume	Metric Volume
Baking or Cake Pan (square or rectangular)	8×8×2	20×20×5	8 cups	2 L
	9×9×2	23×23×5	10 cups	2.5 L
	13×9×2	33×23×5	12 cups	3 L
Loaf Pan	8½×4½×2½	21×11×6	6 cups	1.5 L
	9×9×3	23×13×7	8 cups	2 L
Round Layer Cake Pan	8×1½	20×4	4 cups	1 L
	9×1½	23×4	5 cups	1.25 L
Pie Plate	8×1½	20×4	4 cups	1 L
	9×1½	23×4	5 cups	1.25 L
Baking Dish or Casserole			1 quart/4 cups	1 L
			1½ quart/6 cups	1.5 L
			2 quart/8 cups	2 L
			3 quart/12 cups	3 L